# "STRANGE PARALLEL"

## ZEBULUN — THE NETHERLANDS

## A TRIBE OF ISRAEL

BY

## HELENE W. KOPPEJAN

ZEBULUN HYMN by NIEK SCHEPS

ORIGINAL SKETCHES BY BARBARA ALLEN TOBECKSEN

PUBLISHER

**ARTISAN PUBLISHERS**
P.O. Box 1529
Muskogee, Oklahoma 74402
(918) 682-8341
www.artisanpublishers.com

American Edition Revised From 2nd Edition Book "Strange Parallel"

ISBN: 0-93466-13-X
LIBRARY OF CONGRESS CATALOG CARD NUMBER: 83-73689

1

All geographical names mentioned in the book are indicated on this map

Drawing W. A. Koppejan

# CONTENTS

# FORWARD

Was I led "by chance" to Zebulun Hove in Glastonbury? I also used to ask myself was I led by chance to become an archaeologist, writer and publisher. But I have since realized I had no choice! My personal belief is that the daily events in one's life are just cogs in the wheel of Destiny, when one is cognizant that God controls our destiny.

What appeared to have been a chance remark mentioned a film purported to identify the Netherlands with one of the so-called Ten Lost Tribes in Israel that disappeared in Assyrian captivity. The film had been produced by a Dutch family living in Glastonbury, England. I immediately went to Glastonbury where I met a fellow researcher in a subject I had been studying for many years. What a thrill to meet Helene Koppejan whose painstaking research I found contributed so much to my understanding of the Dutch people.

A major portion of my research and writings concerned the history of the Israelites as revealed from Assyrian clay cuneiform tablets of their sojourn in captivity and their eventual migrations westward. Archaeology has confirmed the identification of the Anglo-Saxon, Scandinavian, Germanic, Celtic and kindred peoples as descendants of the Lost Tribes of Israel and have actually identified some of the tribes with certain modern nations. However, it is imperative that all the ten tribes be found and identified today to confirm the Old Testament prophecies and awaken all Israelites to their heritage and destiny.

Helene had not only produced a film on the strange parallel between the Netherlands and Zebulun, a tribe of Israel, but also a book on the same subject. I had wondered in the past about the possibility of the Dutch being of Zebulun because of Jacob's blessing on Zebulun. These prophetic blessings made reference to ships and the Dutch were one of the greatest maritime nations of modern history. After viewing the film "Strange Parallel" I was firmly convinced the Dutch were predominantly of the tribe of Zebulun.

Helene shared my desire that her work be made available to the people of the United States, many of whom are of Dutch descent, and graciously gave me permission to publish this American edition of her book "Strange Parallel."

E. Raymond Capt

5

Signboard
Zebulun Hove,
Real Israel Press,
55 Hill Head,
Glastonbury,

## PREFACE

At last, Strange Parallel, you go forward into the world! May you travel fast into the heart of the right readers. "At last" said I, because I studied the subject for more than ten years. At last "fast," I say now, having written this book within a couple of weeks. It all of a sudden was given to me in the sequence of Zebulun being mentioned in the Bible. I wrote it almost in my sleep in the early morning-hours.

Of course the purpose of the book is to draw your attention towards my country, Holland, in a completely new way never heard of so far. As such it is written for those who are interested in another people or may be even their own ancestors, the Dutch.

The main aim is to arouse interest for a completely new kind of reading the Bible. People have told me that I am introducing an entirely new principle which has been the result of my systematic research. The principle itself is very simple: I read a name in the Bible and I started to make lists of all the references to this particular word in different Concordances (James Strong and Gesenius). I then laid the verses alongside the culture of my own country and its history. Soon I began to realise I had to learn Hebrew myself.

I got the chance to attend the lessons of the Jewish Professor F. Weinreb in Holland during 1964-1968, years in which I was being taught the deeper meaning of the Hebrew words and their letters being numbers. Thus for instance it came to me how Zebulun's Hebrew letters might symbolize one of our national treasures: the water-windmills.

One may see how the results of my research fit in like a jigsaw-puzzle, following the sequence of the Biblical Books as they have been handed down in the English James version and the Dutch Statenbijbel. What I have written down is only a first start showing the main headlines. There being many more sub-titles such as the meaning of Zebulun's sons and the names of the cities in Zebulun's territory, I have left them out in this first approach. I hope it is enough for the reader to get a first glimpse of the blueprint the Creator gave to a strangely interlaced circle of peoples and each individual born within it to be gathered back into Israel.

I hardly realise myself that I have been delving into something new. To me it came in such a logical sequence and I don't understand why others did not find it long before me. It seems however as if the time was not ripe until now to be given the Light that a Biblical name, a son of Jacob, (one of a circle of twelve, being the symbolic number of earthly completion which is to be found everywhere in the cosmos) can be laid word for word and meaning for meaning in all its Hebrew implications alongside the character and the culture and the history and the geography and even the language of a people in North Western Europe, having nothing to do with the Jews but with their lost ten brothers.

In the parallel between Zebulun and Holland mind and matter or the spiritual and the physical world become one again. As such this study is only a start. Others may take over the lamp with the light that has been thrown on Holland and Zebulun first, which in itself will be a remarkable proof of Isaiah's prophecy on the light in Zebulun's land dealt with in the text.

I am indebted to E. Raymond Capt for his intiative to get my book revised and published for the American readers. My special greeting and blessing go with this book to all friends of American-Dutch descent. May this book enlighten your identity with the heritage of a small but great nation—Holland.

January 1984                                           Helene Koppejan
                          Zebulun-Hove
                    55 Hill Head,  Glastonbury,
                    Somerset,  Great   Britain
                          (BA6 8AW)

# CHAPTER 1.

## HOLLAND IDENTIFIED WITH ZEBULUN, A NEW IDEA?

You had probably never heard of this identification. It may strike you as strange. It is indeed quite a new idea. Indeed it took wings only recently and has already roused interest in Anglo-Dutch-Danish quarters, which prompted me to write this booklet, containing thē results of my investigations. The novelty of the idea is apparent from parts which deal with the Biblical background and the research work involved. It shows quite a new approach to the subject. A systematic analysis of a Biblical tribe of Israel and its comparison with a north-western European country with a national culture has never before been undertaken. As such it is original.

The identification of one of Israel's tribes with a country and a particular nation is not new. At Hoorn, north of Amsterdam, there are three 17th century step-gabled houses with a decorated frieze showing the battle of the Dutch at Hoorn against the Spanish Admiral Bossu. The houses are now called Bossu-Huizen with inscriptions saying that the Hollander identify themselves with *Israel* and the Spanish with *Amalek*, who is always Israel's antagonist in the Bible.

One inscription reads:

> *„O, loffelijke daed. O! schoone gulde tijden!*
> *Wie dat er aen gedenckt, die moet hem nog verblijden,*
> *Het land dat schut, en beeft, den vijand die komt aen;*
> *Hij wil met Amelak gantsch Israel verslaen.*
> *Hij koomt met groote magt, maer Godt heeft ons gegeven*
> *Ook arons ende hurs [1]) wiens namen zijn geschreven."*

"Oh glorious deed, oh golden times,
who ever thinks of them, he is rejoicing still,
the land that shakes and trembles, the enemy
is nearing fast,
he will with Amalek all Israel defeat, he comes
with greatest might,
But God has given *us* Aarons, even Hurs,
whose names are written.

In that "golden" 17th century when the Dutch had won the battle for religious (Protestant) freedom, they were conscious of being literally Israel. They were enlightened Bible-readers.

The 17th century "Chronicle of Zealand" by Smallegange (see page 86 ) shows how historians in those days were convinced that the early inhabitants of the Netherlands, the Batavians, the

Frisians, the Menapians and others were descended from the Hebrews and father Noah.

For generations the British have noticed a parallel between Ephraim and England, Manassah and the United States, Dan and Denmark. Although a vast literature exists about it in English, no publication exists of a systematic study comparing the Biblical aspects word for word with a modern country, showing parallels from a historic, geographic, socio-psychological, cultural and symbolic aspect.

This study is a very first attempt at starting a new kind of research and creating fresh interest in these strange parallels, which may be called hypotheses or inner visions, or..just pure nonsense. If a reader comes to the latter conclusion he would have to prove that it is indeed non-sense. Until then my view is just as valid as his, with this important difference that I have studied the subject for many years.

Trying to launch a new idea, unheard of by most readers, it is difficult to make a choice from the vast storehouse of wisdom existing in British libraries about the Anglo-Saxon-Celtic peoples being descended from the ancient House in Israel, (as distinguished from the Jews) and the vision that the personal identification with the restoration of the Kingdom of Israel (not to be identified with the modern State of Israel) will have its origin within the nucleus of these cultures. In what follows I have hardly scratched the surface of this enormous amount of material.

Before The Light returns to restore the earth we have to know ourselves and our identities, not only as individuals but also as peoples. This will serve as a passport for entry into the coming new age in which purified Israel with twelve different 'tribes' will once again form the twelve gates of Jerusalem.

This strange-sounding pronouncement is based on the strong faith that we in our present generation have to guard as a pearl of great value all that has been passed on to us by previous generations who have ruled with God and have been enlightened by His Spirit.

I hope, therefore, that this first study of parallels may be followed by systematic research into eleven other equally strange parallels so that we may be able to store up a definite knowledge of what we now only see as a dim light in the distance during the years in which our countries only seem to be heading towards darkness.

'Holland' and 'The Netherlands' have been used as interchangeable names. Strictly speaking 'The Netherlands' is the King-dom's official name. (Kroninkrijk der Nederlanden)   The name 'Holland' is more familiar, specially in the States although the name only applies to the two coastal provinces of North and South Holland. The old geographical name 'the Lowlands' is of ancient historical origin and comprises the coastal area of both Belgium and Holland.

## JOHN WILSON IDENTIFIED HOLLAND WITH ZEBULUN

In 1837 a theologian from Cambridge, John *Wilson*, started lecturing all over the British Isles and continued doing so until his death in 1870. His main subjects were the Israelitish origin of the Anglo-Saxon-Celtic peoples, the Davidic descent of the British Royal Family, the Hebrew origin of North-West European lan-guages, the difference between the Lost House of Israel (in Western Europe) and the Jews of Judah, who at the time were dispersed all over the world.

According to later reports his lectures were timely and they became very popular in England.   Clergymen, schoolmasters, rabbis, even Queen Victoria herself became interested.   However Wilson himself said: "Let us work with patience and hope for the rising generation; it always takes a generation for any newly dis-covered truth to take root and spring up, as this must evidently do ."

Regarding his vision that Holland was to be identified with Zebulun, Jacob's son, it took more than a hundred years before this truth began to take root in Holland! Strangely enough this subject failed to receive the attention of British researchers into Anglo-Saxon-Celtic-Israel origins, although a storehouse of books, magazines and lectures about the other ideas launched by Wilson, is now in existence and available in English-speaking countries.

## A CENTURY LATER, A CHALLENGE IN HOLLAND

When in Canada, just after having graduated from Amsterdam University in social sciences and feeling well-informed, I was asked in all sincerity to which tribe of Israel the Dutch belonged. I simply could not answer the strange question. It became a challenge and I hope it will have the same effect on you, dear reader. It was either sheer folly connecting a figure in the Bible with the national character of one's own nation and thus reversing the present trend towards internationalism and one-worldism or it would be a fascina-ting discovery. I saw in a flash that all my scattered academical knowledge could be integrated for the purpose of one fascinating research project. I took up the challenge and the idea became more than a strange parallel to me.

Back in Holland in 1958 I talked about this idea of Holland being Zebulun with Willem Koppejan, who at the time was a medical-psychological consultant of repute at The Hague. To my surprise he lent me a book, written by a Dutchman in 1920, J.A.F. Moerzer Bruyns at the League of Nations in Geneve, writing about the psychology of nations. In this rather odd book with some extreme views he mentioned however that Holland was Zebulun!

Willem Koppejan told me he himself was convinced about Holland's identity with Zebulun-Cancer. He however did not have the time to go deeper into the subject. This convinced me more than anything else of being on the right track and it prompted me to start my independent research. The reward came, when this same Willem asked me to marry him in March '70.

The first articles in Holland about Zebulun were published in the journal "Een Nieuw Geluid" (Striking a New Note) in 1962. This is the monthly *magazine* of the "Bond Nederlands Israel." (Association Netherlands-Israel) Evert *Smit*, the former Editor of this magazine replied to my article as he happened to have arrived at the same conclusion but from a different angle. He specially mentioned the "light-prophecy" in connection with Zebulun in Holland for which I am indebted to him. Here then were "two witnesses" to carry on our research. The idea caught on and resulted in quite a few Dutchmen calling themselves Zebulunites, considering it a blessing and a shield against the arrows of a new moral. What is in a name? It might become a life-saver! Some have approached me with the request for further details as to Zebulun's identification with Holland. I hope that this booklet will fill this need for the time being.

Now, please get a Bible and follow me to those places where Zebulun is mentioned both in Hebrew and in Greek from Genesis to Revelation so as to investigate what they may mean.

A hundred years ago John Wilson sowed a seed. May Prince Zebulun come soon to wake his beautiful sleeping princess Holland.

# CHAPTER 2.

## WHO WAS ZEBULUN?

In the first book of the Bible, Genesis 30:20, an account of his birth is given. Zebulun is the youngest son of Jacob's (the patriarch) marriage to Leah (the matriarch), being the sixth son. His elder brothers are Reuben, Simeon, Levi, Judah and Issaschar.

Although being the youngest son Zebulun must have enjoyed the same education as these elder brothers of Leah's household. There were half-brothers as well, children of Jacob's wives maids. Their names were Asher, Dan, Gad and Naphtali. Their mothers being bondswomen, suggests that these did not possess the outspoken characters of Leah's and Rachel's children. Jacob loved Leah's younger sister Rachel. He had been tricked by their father, Jacob's uncle Laban, who had given him Leah instead of Rachel on his wedding night. Leah had given him children but Rachel was still barren although Joseph was to be born soon after Zebulun. Leah, the tender-eyed, was not loved but she still hoped that Jacob would finally "dwell" with her. In this mood she named her sixth son and said:

> "God has endued me with a good dowry, now will my husband *dwell* with me, because I have born him six sons, and she called him ZEBULUN."

This Hebrew word means: *to inclose, to reside, to dwell.*
It is composed of three Hebrew letters:

*Zain* meaning fish-hook, *hook*
*Beith* meaning house, *home,* dwelling
*Lamed* meaning *movement,* streaming, impulse to action.

Z..B..L... The Dwelling
   —which hooks up water
   —with the movement

Although the name Zebulun was chosen for the purpose of calling Jacob home to Leah, this wish remained unfulfilled. Zebulun was her last son. Rachel became pregnant and gave him a son called Joseph, a fruitful bough who was destined to become Pharoah's right hand in Egypt. Soon after Jacob fled from Laban his father in law with all his household and cattle.

Standing before the promised homeland Canaan, he struggled with an angel, was blessed and given a new name by him: Israel, meaning "as a prince ruling with God who hast power."

All this happened when *Zebulun and Joseph* were under seven years old. It is well known that experiences gained during the first seven years leave a marked impression on one's adult life.

## CLOSE FRIENDSHIP BETWEEN ZEBULUN AND JOSEPH

Although the Bible does not tell us, we may assume, that it must have made a deep and lasting impression on these youngest sons (Benjamin was still to come) that their father Jacob got a lame hip overnight, and changed his and consequently their name into Israel!

Their reaction must have been quite different to that of their eldest brother Reuben, then already a grown-up man, who had defiled his father's bed!

In *"The Testament of the Patriarchs"* a very plausible story is told about Zebulun and Joseph, demonstrating their close friendship:

When the Patriarch Zebulun is lying on his deathbed he tells his sons how Joseph was sold by his brothers. After having related how his elder brothers wished to kill Joseph, he mentions how he as the only one pleaded with tears for his brother Joseph's life and how his heart pounded and he was unable to stand.

"And when Joseph saw me weeping with him, and them coming against him to slay him, he fled behind me, beseeching them."
The brothers sold Joseph to the Ishmaelites, but Zebulun warns his sons, saying: "In his price, I had no share, my children!" Because, when he was crying for Joseph who was thrown into a pit, he had been set as a watch over him, and Zebulun had been crying with and talking to Joseph.

"I'm not conscious that I have sinned all my days save in thought, not yet do I remember that I have done any iniquity, *except the sin of ignorance which I committed against Joseph,* for I covenanted with my brethren not to tell my father what had been done."

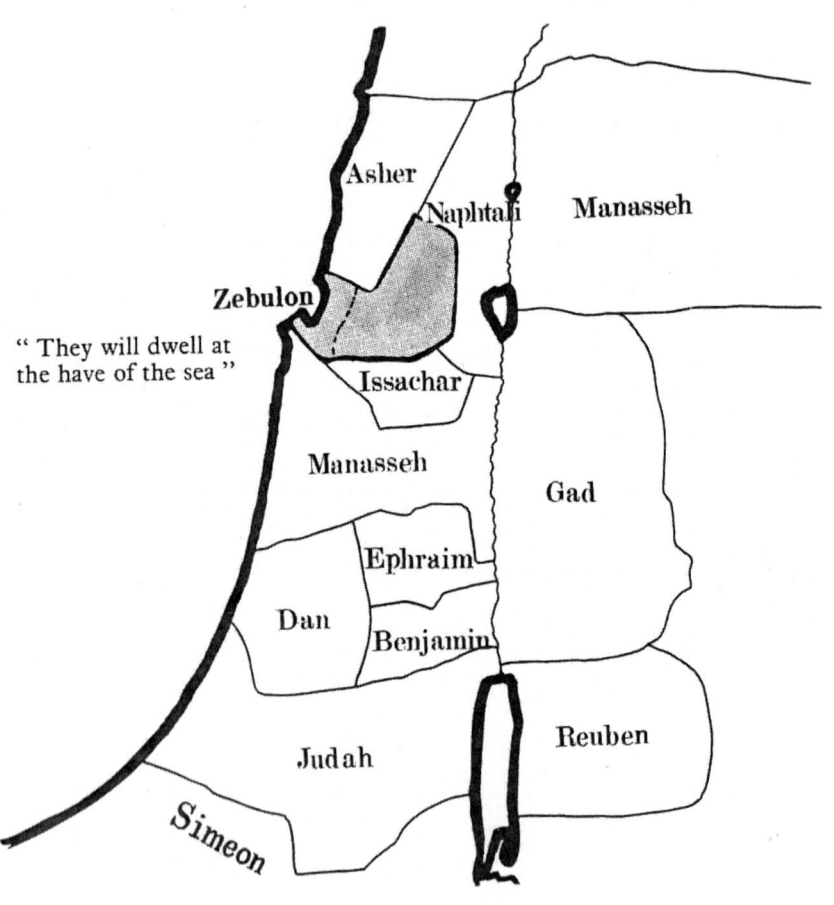

Asher

Naphtali

Manasseh

Zebulon

" They will dwell at
the have of the sea "

Issachar

Manasseh

Gad

Ephraim

Dan

Benjamin

Judah

Reuben

Simeon

TRIBAL LANDS IN ANCIENT ISRAEL

## BRITAIN AND THE NETHERLANDS
## "CANNOT WITHOUT THE OTHER"

Taking for granted for a moment that the Netherlands are identifiable with Zebulun, and Britain with Joseph (whose children Ephraim symbolize England and Manasseh North America), one only has to have a glance at the history of these two peoples since Roman times to notice that *basically,* they look the same, they talk the same way, they have more or less the same mental outlook, they share the same interests, and they have always had the same common enemies, although forefathers of the Dutch (the Batavians) as Roman soldiers were set to watch over Britannica, and although the English and the Dutch have fought their brotherly sea-battles, and although the Boer-war in South Africa made a deep scar. Still it is in comparison with what other peoples did to each other, as close a friendship as Zebulun had with Joseph. For the future we may certainly remember the words of Queen Elizabeth I in the 16th century about England and the Netherlands:

'THE ONE CANNOT WITHOUT THE OTHER'

## THE PATRIARCH ZEBULUN, A DECENT MAN,
## ( DR. A. VAN SELMS. )

We know very little about the man Zebulun from the Bible. Unlike his brothers, he did not do anything spectacular.

A Dutch theologian, Dr. A. *van Selms,* wrote a book in Dutch, "Living Past," exclusively about Zebulun and he made a special trip to Israel to describe all the historical spots and places associated with Zebulun. This is a remarkable study by a Dutchman, and although he does not give us the slightest hint ever to have heard about the identity of Holland with Zebulun, he gives us food for thought.

Van Selms stresses the fact that in contrast to his brothers, *nothing evil or wrong doing can be said of Zebulun and his tribe:* He was unlike Reuben, who defiled his father's bed, unlike Levi, who plundered and murdered, unlike Judah who took "the harlot" and gave her his ring and staff, unlike the Ephraimites who became drunkards, unlike Manasseh's tribe worshipping idols, unlike Dan slaying people with the sword and burning them, unlike Asher and Naphtali preferring to live amongst the degenerated Canaanites.

Only about Issaschar and Zebulun nothing wrong has been mentioned. When realizing, that up till the present time no evil could be told about this Prince Zebulun and his descendents, Dr. van Selms writes, that he continuously hears singing in him, while walking thirty kilometers a day, in his sixtieth year, over the ancient territory of Zebulun, "No evil from Zebulun, not in the Bible, not now in the present."

Isn't it strange that in 1965 this Dutch Reformed clergyman was so happy with this discovery, that his heart began to sing? Why did this Hollander choose Zebulun of all twelve patriarchs to write a book about? Pure chance? Unconscious intuition that the Dutch have some kind of relationship with the Israel tribe of Zebulun? Or is he unconsiously bearing as a blind witness to being a Zebulunite himself? Or again, is it just a strange parallel, that a Protestant Dutch Doctor of theology, was the only one so far to write a study about Prince Zebulun and his former territory?

Anyhow he stresses the fact that Zebulun was a decent man, the most peaceful patriarch, full of compassion, and that his tribe was the happiest one of all the twelve.

### THE DUTCH, A PEACEFUL PEOPLE

What can be said about the Dutch throughout the ages? In comparison with other powers in the world they have indeed played a peaceful rule. Was it mere accident that the International Court of Justice (the Peace-Palace) was chosen to be built at The Hague, right in the parliamentary heart of Holland?

Although the Dutch were by no means suckers they have only fought *defensive wars* when others have invaded their territory. The Romans in the first century, the Vikings with their raids in the Middle Ages, the Spaniards with their objectionable religion in the 16th century, while the French under Napoleon took the country without resistance, as the Germans almost did in our own time. Against both the latter Regimes the Dutch fought back more mentally than physically.

On the whole they have not been aggressors, apart of course from the fact that individual Dutchmen helped to slaughter Indians, sold negroes as slaves and bred revolts in their former colonies. The innate folk-character of the Dutch favors peaceful families and clean dwellers.

Moreover the Dutch frequently have functioned as a *buffer-state* for Britain against agression from other nations. Often the visible results seemed small, and like at the time of Zebulun when he was watching over Joseph in the pit, there was weeping, trembling, a pounding of heart and inability to remain standing upright, though mentally in accord with John Bull.

## ZEBULUN'S TESTAMENT

The traditional (Hebrew) manuscript dating from the last century B.C. "The Testament of the Twelve Patriarchs," gives an account of Zebulun's spiritual legacy to his children:

"Have *compassion* to all as I did on account of Joseph."

"I made *a catch of fish* for Jacob my father, and *when many were choked in the sea, I continued unhurt.*"

"I was *the first to make a boat to sail* upon the sea, for the Lord gave me understanding and wisdom therein."

*"Through compassion I shared* my catch *with every stranger."*

"Have therefore yourselves also, my children, *compassion* towards everyman with mercy...because also in the last days God will send His compassion on the earth, and wheresoever he findeth bowels of mercy, He dwelleth in him."

*"observe the waters* and *know when they flow together*...if they are divided into many streams, the earth swalloweth them up and they become of no account. Be ye not therefore divided into two heads..."

The Patriarch prophecizes concerning his posterity: They will be divided in Israel, they shall follow two kings, and shall work abomination, and their enemies shall lead them captive..after these things shall they remember the Lord and repent...but again they shall provoke Him to anger, and they shall be cast away until the time of the consummation.

Could there be something of a sad parallel, in that the "southern-Netherlands," the Dutch speaking parts of Belgium are under a different king, and their northern brothers by the Spaniards, the French and the Germans? And isn't there also a divided mentality among the tribe themselves?

The last words of the Patriarch to his sons before he falls asleep at the good old age of one hundred and fourteen years, are:

"For I shall rise again in the midst of you, as a ruler in the midst of his sons; and I shall rejoice in the midst of my tribe, as many as shall keep the law of the Lord, and the commandments of Zebulun their father. But upon the ungodly shall the Lord bring (eternal) fire, and destroy them throughout all generations."

Not much more is known about Zebulun apart from the Bible. From the other semi-apocryphal books we don't get better informa-

19

tion than what we find in the Bible. So let us turn to that Book again and search if there is anything in the blessings given to Zebulun and the Netherlands.

It has sometimes been argued by English fellow researchers that Holland's status of elder brother compared to Ephraim — England's is significant and that Holland therefore should be identified with Manasseh, Joseph's eldest Son. However so far I have not found any indications of similarity so as to identify Manasseh with Holland while on the contrary the point of this book is that Zebulun-identity-marks are legion. My British friends have sustained my thesis, by stressing the "elderly brother position" towards Britain in our Dutch history. However the parallel is: Zebulun-Holland as the elder brother of Joseph-Britain. This is a subject in itself and in this study no further comparisons will be made with other tribes.

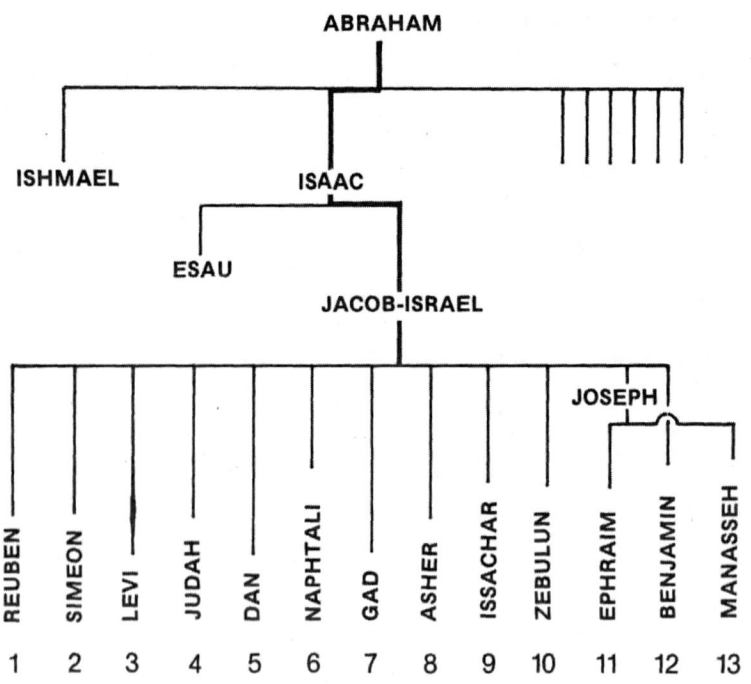

ISRAEL'S THIRTEEN TRIBES

20

# CHAPTER 3.

## A MEANING BEHIND ZEBULUN

In a dictionary or concordance, you will find the word Zebulun to mean dwelling, habitation, enclosure. However the Hebrew text can be translated and understood on different levels. There is a spiritual meaning, but also an "outer" and "inner" historical one. Then again there is a more material translation and even a counterfeit-translation of the word itself possible, showing what will happen if the high spiritual meaning within the word is not lived up to.

As to these deeper meanings of the words, the Hebrew word in itself is a magnificent creation and living up to it is far beyond us. A thorough study of Hebrew is necessary to receive back a different mentality. We in the modern western world have lost the inner meaning of words, let alone being guided by them. Every word nowadays must be clearly informative without a double meaning so that it can be fed into a computer. Not so in Hebrew. In good books there are no wrong translations of Hebrew either, only different levels that may not make sense if intermixed, which has often been the cause of theological wars.

However in this coming age of symbols, we shall have to re-discover the different levels of meaning of Biblical words and sentences and re-learn how to combine. We are quickly losing the ability of "playing upon words," for which the English language is still fitted best, and even the pun is nowadays seen as a lower from of wit. Not so in the Bible, in one word an entire story can be told.

This book is a first attempt to show what may be hidden in the word Zebulun and what is told about him. However every word may be elaborated on and you, dear reader, may still find other levels of interpretation, but you will have to study Hebrew to achieve it.

Take the word Zebulun in the meaning of dwelling-culture. As Dr. van Selms shows us, it also means "*the elevated*," the one who has been lifted up. This reminds him of the Lowlands' story, that the future Batavian chief Brinio, when born, was elevated on a shield to be shown.

It reminds me of the ancient custom by the Dutch, when Hollands' princes were elevated shortly after birth and shown to the people. Strange isn't it, that this seemed to be an old particularly *Dutch* custom, reminding us of the name Zebulun!

21

This is as it were a more spiritual meaning than the word "dwelling." On the other hand, following again Dr. van Selms in this, the counterfeit translation of the word is also revealing: *Beelzebul* the only combined meaning in which the word Zebulun is used, which became the symbol for the lord of the flies and the devil. (Matthew 10:25; 12:24-28)

However, it means literally "Lord of Zebulun" and as such used as "the Lord of the house or dwelling," or the household idol Baal. According to Dr. van Selms the word Zebulun (in Ugarit) may mean "sickness," and as such it is used by Jesus when the possessed are healed by him. *He is driving out Beelzebul, who has caused the sickness.* (Matthew 12:24-29) (see note page 95)

## DUTCH DWELLING—CULTURE

If therefore we see a strange parallel between Zebulun and Dutch dwelling-culture, between Holland and Zebulun, we should not be too much given to laudations that this small nation are all of Israel. Who can judge? Individually and nationally is a question of *who* is entering as the Lord of the House, the one who causes sickness, polluted air, water and unclean thinking (new morals) in our homes, or the one who brings the true Light, whose feet walked upon the territory of Zebulun.

Revelation 7:8 speaks of a future when twelve thousand Zebulunites, who will be sealed on their forehead, because they did not bow their head to Baal, will escape the plagues. Is this to be taken in a merely symbolical sense or in a more literal one, too gruesome to think of? or are the "12,000" the leaders being gathered out of Zebulun first? Who is going into his inner dwelling to welcome the Light? By cleaning the house and by a new birth we will be elevated as princes of Israel. That is the high calling of "Hollands Binnenhuis," the Dutch interior.

"Of the continental peoples, the Dutch are most like the British. They are optimistic, share a liking for quiet off-beat humor, and are friendly and reserved as the mood takes them. *Their lives revolve around their comfortable homes, for the Dutch believe houses are built to be made into homes.* They will be quick to point out that *they were the people who invented the idea* at a time when the rest of the world seemed content with four walls, a roof, a handkerchief sized window for light and air. They could be right, for *in the 17th century architects from all over Europe went to Holland to copy domestic architecture.*"
(Collins - Tourist guide, London '68, page 8)

23

Indeed the Dutch have been famous for their interiors throughout the ages, claiming to have invented decoration. Famous Dutch paintings of the 16th-17th centuries show "Hollands Binnenhuis" and its unique atmosphere, of which the highly emancipated Dutch woman was the vital centre, as many a foreigner in those days has described. Rembrandt, Pieter de Hoogh, Vermeer painted rich Dutch family scenes and interiors with light streaming through stained glass windows coloring the white and black tiles, the decorated walls, carved oak, beautiful china, copper utensils and magnificent arrangements of flowers, step gabled houses with winding staircases (a Dutch invention) along clean Dutch canals. Dutch family dwellings were later imitated by other countries — Denmark, South Africa and the early settlers in America.

And not only in the past! The Dutch are even now renowned for their home making. They like large windows, open curtains at night, which surprises the tourist, showing lots of lamps and lights (advertising Philips light bulbs!) Going through Holland by train at night gives the traveller an impression of homeliness and life in the Dutch dwellings different from Belgium, France and other European countries.

It is an established fact that the Dutch spend their spare time not so much in pubs, cafes and coffee houses but in their homes. Children do their home work at home, they hardly ever go to boarding schools. Businessmen, politicians take their files home with them to work on in the evening. Television is in almost every Dutch home, and here I have to strike a discordant note: Dutch family life nowadays and Dutch mentality are at present more influenced by television programs than those of any other nationality. This also means that the "Lord of the Home" may enter through the TV set. For better for worse. There is a lot of unclean thinking going on in Dutch homes nowadays and Holland is already "famous" for its rapid increase in new sex-relationships practised within the cosy intimacy of small family circles and home parties. Dutch dwelling-culture, also in an advanced state of degeneration, tends to making the homes divided against themselves. Enclosure, in what?! And yet, the enclosed, fenced in house, with a garden or "hof" is so typically Dutch and a mark of Zebulun.

The Dutch have to build "elevated houses." Their houses are all built on sand, clay and mud, as there is not rock underneath Holland's soil. So they have to be built on piles. The entire city of Amsterdam has been built on piles: *an elevated city with a Dutch ancient dwelling-culture,* and of contrast, still *below sea level.*

As one of the examples of "Dwelling-culture," which is advanc-

25

ing and becoming an example for the rest of the world too, is the fact that almost every Dutch town or village has its *preservation society* for the conservation of their architectural beauty. Moreover there are many national Trusts and Societies, who are doing great work guarding entire towns and villages against demolition.

# CHAPTER 4.

## INTRODUCING THE BLESSINGS FOR ZEBULUN

The so-called Blessings in the Bible are given to the twelve tribes of Israel on several occasions. They are some sort of predictions or prophecies concerning the tribe and one would nowadays call them a character-analysis of talents, which, if lived up to its high calling, will bear fruit, and which according to Jacob, Moses and Deborah, who utter them will be blessed. However there seems to be the condition: to live according to the inheritance of the congregation of Jacob (Israel) (Gen. 49 : 13) and to the law commanded by Moses. (Deuteronomy 33 : 4)

It seems to me that these blessings provide a strange parallel with peoples within the "lost" ten tribes, now among the Anglo-Saxon-Celtic nations, if they, although blind to their own identity, have, at least, tried to live up to Christian standards. However I believe we have seen, that the blessings given to a certain tribe (of which we see a parallel in our modern times) may become if reversed, a special curse, a self willed curse, if they do not live up to their high special calling. I shall give you examples in the next chapters, in which the curse may sometimes be more obvious than the blessing, as the good does not boast, while the evil makes a noise.

There are three "circles" of blessings around each tribe. When you throw a stone in the water it gives different ripples. Compare the name of the tribe with a stone (which in a double sense one may do, see page 41), then the first strong ripple around it is Jacob's blessing to the *son* himself. The second ripple describes a wider circle: Moses giving his blessing to the *tribe* of Israel, while the third ripple around the stone seems to comprise a still wider circle: *the children* of the tribe. As regards Zebulun we are dealing here with the following blessings:

1) *Jacob's* blessing:

> Zebulun *shall dwell at the haven of the sea.* He shall be (for) an haven of ships and his border shall be unto Zidon.
>
> Genesis 49 : 13

2) *Moses'* blessing:

> Rejoice, Zebulun, in thy going out. They shall call the people unto the mountain, there they shall offer sacrifices of righteousness, for *they shall suck of the abundances of the seas and of the treasures hid in the sand.*
>
> Deuteronomy 33 : 18-19

3) *Deborah's* blessing:

> *Zebulun wielding the writer's pen,* a people that risked their lives unto death.

Judges 5 : 14

These blessings are our central theme, completed with:

4) *Isaiah's prophecy:*

> He lightly *afflicted the land* of Zebulun *by way of the sea,* but afterwards brought hono r . (by way of the sea) *The people that walked in darkness have seen a great light.*

Isaiah 9 : 1, 2

5) First Fulfillment:

> (in the land of Zebulun) to them which sat in the region and shadow of death, *light is sprung up.*

Matthew 4 : 13, 15-16

6) Revelation to *John:*

> Hurt not the earth, neither the sea nor the trees, till we have sealed the servants of our God in their foreheads. Of the tribe of Zabulun were *sealed* twelve thousand.

Revelation 7 : 3, 8

Can you see a movement in time, as a stone making ripples in the water makes a wider and wider circle towards the end of times?

I see another comparison and I would like you to reflect upon it: The most important and central point is the birth of a word, a name, in our case Zebulun. It is the *Ego* of each son of Israel. To me Jacob's blessing principally concerns the future status, the tribe to *be,* the father foresees their *Higher being,* how they will be blessed by their innate character.

The second blessing, four hundred years later, when Moses is standing before the Promised Land is to the tribe of 57,400 grown up "warriors," (apart from their households) a full grown tribe of Zebulun, and these blessings are characteristic of what the tribe will be *doing, their achievements,* their way of working by which the tribe may be identified by others in that future.

The third blessing is in the Promised Land and uttered by a woman, the prophetic judge Deborah. Her blessing is more in the nature of an "epitheton ornans," an honored title, being their *prophetically given task to serve* or spiritual part of fortune within the Kingdom of Israel.

In all these three instances the blessing to Zebulun is within the wider scopes of the blessings to all the twelve.

29

The prophet Isaiah however is speaking about the *land* of Zebulun, or that part of the earth on which it will become visible. In his days the tribe was already in exile as we shall see. It is the earthern vessel.

What I endeavour to show you now is that Zebulun and its ripples of blessings, has a strange parallel with Holland, its blessings, (and their possible reversals) i.e its characteristic being, its renown for what it is doing, its best talents, and its low land.

# CHAPTER 5.

## JACOB'S BLESSINGS TO ZEBULUN: A HAVEN

Verse 49 : 13 in Genesis is one of the keys for finding similarities between Zebulun and Holland. There is first of all the name Zebulun which as we have seen means dwelling, and the Dutch as refined dwellers.

Where is that blessed spot in which they will dwell? It is at the haven, or at the seashore. The old Dutch translation (Pieter Keur) even reads:

*"Zebulun shall have his dwellings at the seashore,*
*shall be a haven for a fishing fleet*
*and at his flank he shall catch fish."*

What is actually said here? Zebulun's territory will not be like that of Joseph in everlasting hills. He will not dwell in ships, as is the future of Dan. No, it must needs be a calm seashore with natural harbors and shelter for a fishing fleet. The dwellings will be along the waterside and at natural havens. They will be blessed there with shoals of fish. Fishery will be their peaceful occupation.

There seems to be a strange paradox in the Bible, because nowhere and never did Zebulun live at the seashore during the period before their dispersion from Palestine. The sand-dune shore (now near Acco) was promised to them, but they never occupied it. Was it however fulfilled outside Palestine?

## ZEBULUN AS ONE OF THE LOST TEN TRIBES DISPERSED AND "LOST."

Here I have to insert a little note to make sure that you understand what happened in the 7th century B.C. The ten tribes were banished from Israel through Assyrian deportations, and after Assyria itself was defeated, they started a slow mass migration through central Europe and by way of the Mediterranean Sea Towards the north-west. The tribe of Zebulun must have been part of this westward movement. There is a growing literature pointing out archeologically and through circumstantial evidence, that the highly skilled and cultured peoples (goldsmiths, jewellers) suddenly emerging under names like Scythians, Celts, Cymru and others, are these lost and wandering ten tribes from Israel. (map pg.82 )

Our search for parallels between Holland and Zebulun is based on this "vision."

Into the Lowlands they migrated under such names as Frisians (in the north), Kennemers (Kimren) on the north-west coast, the

31

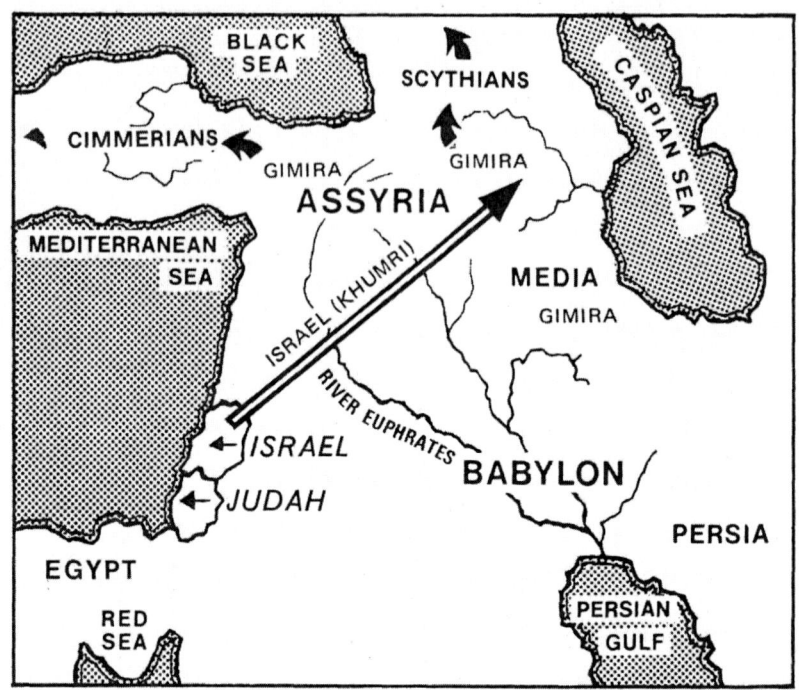

ISRAELITES BECOMING CIMMERIANS AND SCYTHIANS

Batavi along the Rhine, The Katten (Chatti) on the coastal islands, the Kelts and Menapii with the Suevi in the southwest islands, the Saxons in the east of the Lowlands, just to mention a few names.

## HOLLAND AS THE MAIN DELTA OF THE RHINE,

When you have a good look at the map of Western Europe, you see that the Lowlands consist of the greatest delta of Europe formed by the end mouths of three main European rivers, the Rhine from Switzerland through Germany, the Meuse and the Scheldt from France through Belgium. The term Lowlands—used in Roman times—really means all flat land, including Belgian Flanders, which does not imply same as often flooded land. It is not right to suppose that the Netherlands were under water in Roman times. The contrary seems to be true according to recent archeological findings. The great rivers have a calm course into the sea and never rise to such an extent as in subtropical areas.

The catastrophic floods which altered the surface of the lowlands always come from the sea breaking through the natural sand-dune-wall, as has happened in the 5th, the 11th and 14th centuries and as recent as 1953, which gave rise to the so-called Delta-project. Apart from these incidents, it always seems to have been *safe to dwell* there. At least it has often been an overpopulated area, even in Roman times according to their writers. The Lowlands was a gathering place for the "barbaric" tribes, some of whose names I mentioned above, which list is far from complete.

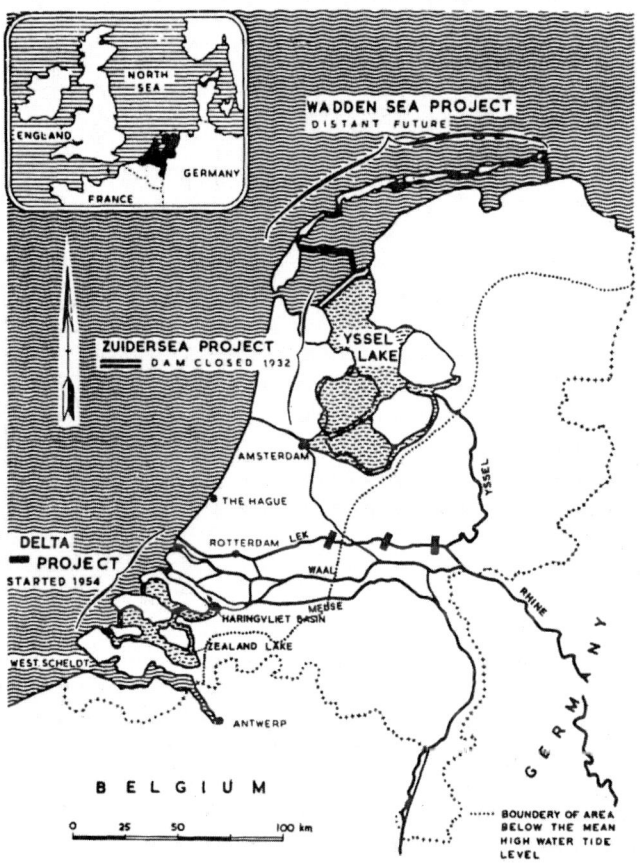

Searching for a natural seashore and natural harbors or haven, nobody can deny, that in the western world, a more natural and safer delta does not exist. Thousands of ships can take refuge, when floating down the rivers or approaching from the sea.

There is not a single rock formation in the Netherlands, and there is hardly any danger due to the almost stagnant waters and the small differences in tides. Moreover the Dutch-Flandrian coast is the *longest range of natural dunes* without rocks in the world,

170 miles, of which the Netherlands form two thirds, while the remainder are man made dykes. Nowhere can one find a more natural parallel with Jacob's blessing to Zebulun!

Don't forget the *climate* either. Holland is blessed with mild winters, it shares the benefit of the Gulfstream, so that fishing and shipping are seldom hindered. Moreover—unless man himself poisons them—there is *not a single poisonous fish* to be found in the waters of the Netherlands both salt and fresh. Every fish may be eaten, apart of course from the unclean fishes forbidden by Israelitish food-laws, a cosmic law, frightfully trespassed against by the average Dutchman, fond of eels, shrimps and oysters, who will only learn the hard way nowadays by contracting peculiar diseases through poisoned shrimps and the other unclean fishes which are at present primarily infected by polluted water. Who invites sickness to his house? You remember the meaning of Baal-Zebul?

Although the geography of the Netherlands is such that every part is now inhabited, thanks to impoldering, geologically speaking the coast is rapidly sinking and losing against the sea since the beginning of this century. Every decade the sand beaches are becoming narrower, and the dunes are "retreating inland." There have been periods that it was the reverse. The rise of the sea in our times is sometimes thought to be alarming, and here we have the strange paradox that living at this seashore as a blessing can also be turned into a curse. Pessimists foretell us that the whole of Holland will be under water, and the queer prophet Nicolaas Kroese saw even the entire capital of Amsterdam inundated because the people were living as in the days of Noah. (He himself died of eating too much) Anyhow it is a fact, that the greater part of *Holland nowadays lies below sea level*, which is unique in itself, realising that on this very spot protected by narrow rows of dunes and man made dykes there lives *the densest population on earth*, being 13 million inhabitants within an area of 12,600 square miles, 110 miles in length from north to south and 110 miles from east to west! Zebulun is the smallest among his brothers, but his quality is not too bad.

It is not often realised that the Rhine, Meuse and Scheldt were *the natural causeways* by which the Israel tribes migrated westward, where on the natural sand and clay delta (one has to dig 120 feet and more and still find no rock) they found refuge and natural harbors to rest before crossing the sea.

Therefore *the Lowlands have always been a transit haven*, and a melting pot of peoples who came to rest from their wanderings.

34

Still, it has *always kept its own characteristic face,* which is a remarkable thing to remember when reflecting on our strange parallel.

## DUTCH DWELLINGS FROM WATTLE AND DAUB, BUILT ON PILES.

Zebulun would live at the seashore. Since pre-historic times the Lowlanders have been inventive and skilled in building. Unlike other regions the Dutch don't possess a single local stone! All their houses had to be built from clay, which they, like the Israelities of old in Egypt, baked (they must have had their own factories as innumerable 'Roman' tiles have been found in the Scheldt area), or, as ancient farms still show, they built from wattle and daub, a skill which eventually they must have brought under the names of "Belgium" tribes into Somerest in Britain! The Lowlanders could never dwell in caves, because these did not exist.

Their dwellings are of brick and wood nowadays still, apart from modern concrete skyscrapers. These last things, which are ugly in the flat land with far horizons ask for special engineering skill, because they tend to sink into the muddy soil.

### DUTCH PILERS

To be a piler ("heier") is a very ancient skilled job in Holland, and now it is a well known Dutch surname "den Heier." All the foundations of most Dutch houses are piles piled deep into the ground. From prehistoric times the Lowlanders have been very advanced in building houses on piles along quays and roads built on wattle and piles. Dutch engineers were often asked for advice and actually built castles and estates in watery areas, as on Fuenen in Denmark (Egeskov) or in England at the Thames, Yarmouth, Cambridge Fens.

The reason for mentioning this is to show that Dutch always have been renowned for building dwellings (Zebulun) in watery areas and alongside haven, ditches, quays and seashore. ( blessing given to Zebulun is to dwell at the seashore and natural harbors )

## A SHIP, ZEBULUN'S SYMBOL AND HOLLANDS' FOLKLORE.

'Zebulun shall be a haven of ship.'' The Hebrew word for ship is *aniah.* It means ship, but also fleet, conveyance, galley, navy. Moreover it means the I.

Strangely enough this word appears here for the first time in the Bible! Were there no ships before Zebulun was born? Of course there were. However especially Zebulun seems to be blessed with the knowledge of ships in haven. As tradition calls him *the first ship builder* with sails, there is no doubt that the blessing extends to shipbuilding in harbors.

"I WAS THE FIRST TO MAKE A BOAT TO SAIL"

According to ancient Hebrew tradition *the banner of Zebulun is always a ship*. The symbols of other tribes are sometimes mixed up, but the one of Zebulun has never been changed. The pictures always show a typical fishing-boat with a sail. Not a rowing-boat or a galley. They may be inspired by fishing boats in the Mediterranean, but the strange thing is that there they look unmistakably like the "pleyte" the fishing boat used in the middle ages and (before) in the Scheldt-area. (Flanders and Zealand) They also look like the old fashioned "boms" used as fishing boats at the South-Holland seashore. They are specially used for sandy, muddy shores and they can easily be pulled ashore.

One would wish the national heraldic symbol of the Netherlands were a ship. Not so! It is a *lion*, and nine out of eleven Dutch provinces have the lion displayed in their coat of arms. One would say this has nothing to do with Zebulun. But wait! Zebulun marched with Issaschar under the banner of Judah, as part of the four squared nation of Israel (Numbers 2 : 7), and Judah's banner is the lion! There is no mean parallel here!

Relatively few Dutch towns have a ship in their crest, although in the middle ages the capital Amsterdam had the symbol of a kof-ship in its seal which is almost identical with the Hebrew drawings of Zebulun's banner.

The Dutch people however made the ship with sails their national folk-symbol. They made it the symbol of their national culture. Look at the ancient *Delft blue tiles*. The ship is predominant on it. Look at Dutch paintings, Dutch embroidery with decorated ships, Dutch silversmiths who engraved and modelled ships, the museums full of ship's models, the ship-weather vanes on towers, ships in churches. This Dutch folk-art has to the same extent only been rivalled by Denmark! What about Dan? His blessing was "abiding in ships." So no wonder they displayed ships in their folk-art. Dan abiding in ships, Zebulun making ships and dwelling at a haven ships. no doubt they were closely connected in Biblical times. Unmistakably Holland and Denmark also share the same cultural heritage. But Dan's banner being a serpent or adder, the

Danish viking ships are a strange parallel to that symbol. The Netherlands are typified by other kinds of ships. Just a few more *examples of exclusive Dutch ship's models:*

The very speedy *flute* or *"flyboat"* (fluit) was invented by the Dutch in the 16th century and this is the historical reason why they became masters of the sea in the 16th century. (Only surpassed by the English in the 17th)

Another Dutch invention was the *tow boat* (trekschuit), being some sort of mailcoach on water, drawn by horses alongside the canals. The larger towns in Holland's flat land had a most efficient regular service in the old days and their timetables could compete with those of modern bus-services frustrated by traffic-jams.

The third Dutch invention was the *herringtube* (haringbuis) with fishing facilities at both "flanks," or sides which as we shall see is very Dutch and of Zebulun too. It is the reason why we Dutch as fishermen are still masters of the Herringpond!

And what about the *"Flying Dutchman?"* Of course you now know it as the symbol of an airline company, but do you realise that the name is taken from the Dutch ghost-ship sailing the seven seas since the 16th century that until recently still scared seamen around the Cape of Good Hope (South Africa) and off the Yorkshire coast? Why is this phantom always called the flying *Dutchman* by sailors and artists all over the world?

Believe it or not as a joke, but our strange parallel between the symbol of a ship for Zebulun and for Holland even has its repercussions in the realms of phantoms and ghosts!!

A ghostly ship, with a ghostly crew,
In tempests she appears;
And before the gale, or against the gale,
She sails without a rag of sail,
Without a helmsman steers.

Longfellow.

**HOLLAND'S FISHER SEAL**

**HOLLAND'S SHIP OF STATE**

The Arms of the Seven provinces are on the side
of the ship, which has the Bible on its prow. The
words (by William the Taciturn) in the circle are:
'Quiet in the midst of the roaring waves'. Poem
at the bottom:

> 'In all pressure and mourning
> Offer each other the hand.
> Be faithful in everything
> God's Church and the Fatherland'

## DIAMOND TRADITIONAL SYMBOL OF ZEBULUN,
## A PARALLEL WITH SOUTH AFRICA AND HOLLAND.

The twelve stones for the twelve tribes of Israel in their right sequence are still a debated subject, due to differences of the original Hebrew text of Exodus 39 : 10-14. However for Zebulun there are no great differences: In the Jewish Encyclopedia, which is based on ancient *Jewish tradition*, the diamond is mentioned as the symbol for Zebulun. I see a parallel here, which might be elaborated when knowing more about gems.

South Africa, the former Dutch settlement, seen as an offshoot from Zebulun, is the land of diamond mining. Almost like a symbol the largest rough diamond has been discovered in South Africa: the Cullinan in *Transvaal* in 1905. This one was sent to *Amsterdam* to be cut and is now part of the crown jewels of England. (Encyclopedia Britannica, nr. 7, page 317, 1960 edition)

*Amsterdam*, the capital of the Netherlands, has since ages been famous for its *diamond-cutting* industry, its cleaving, dividing and setting. This hand process in which generations of mainly Jewish diamond workers of Amsterdam have excelled is still the best. A symbol of Zebulun? Sometimes the pearl has been given as a symbol of Zebulun. This brings me to an even more hidden symbolic parallel.

## THE PEARL AND THE ZODIACAL SIGN OF CANCER,
## TRADITIONAL SYMBOL OF HOLLAND AND ZEALAND.

In Zealand, in the estuary of the Scheldt are the famous oyster-pits, whose oysters have been traded all over Western Europe. On their original natural finding-spots a large industry has flouished until it was decided that the Deltaworks would close the sea-arms. As oysters need fresh tidal waters, the industry is apparently a dying one. Oysters in Zealand are not cultivated for their pearls, because here these are of no value. However the fact that they exist in North-Western Europe is an exceptional one, apart from river pearls found in Scotland. Is it a bit far fetched to bring this in connection with Zebulun?

However there is still another level of symbolic interpretation, which I only mention here, because it is a subject in itself. I just want to call your attention to it: According to ancient folklore and cos-mology *the Netherlands* (especially the coastal part of Holland and Zealand) *"fall under"* *the zodiacal sign of Cancer Crab*. The symbol is connected with the Moon, tides, water, homeliness, shelter, pearls. There are many strange symbolic parallels which *coincide with Zebulun.*

41

## BLESSED WITH A HAVEN FOR FISHFLEET, CATCHING FISH

The Dutch still claim that *a Dutchman invented the method of curing herring* (haringkaken) by a man called Willem Beukelsz from Biervliet in Zealand. The Swedish make the same claim. Anyhow it is a historical fact, that as early as 1320 A.D. the Dutch used a refined method of salting herring by putting them in their ancient natural saltpans (already desired by the Romans!) along the river Scheldt.

CURING HERRING IN THE 18TH CENTURY

Anybody who knows something about the tremendous role the preservation of herring by salting has played during the middle ages

up till recently, will realise that it was indeed a *blessing* meant to save entire populations living in the Celtic fringe of North West Europe: One barrel of salted herrings saved a family of a sea-farers crew from starvation during long winters of sailing the seven seas. Even nowadays the herring is Holland's most popular sea food. Every spring when the new (green) herrings are caught, it is a mad international race between Scottish, Danish, Dutch, Russian and other fishermen as to who will get the first one. After that there is the traditional Dutch race for the first boat of the fleet to be home. The first herringtube back in Holland has the honor of presenting the green herring to the Queen, who of course eats it raw as every good Dutch man and woman does. Ever seen a Dutchman at a fish-stand gulping a herring down his throat? An old left-over custom from Zebulun?

Anyhow it is remarkable that the fishing port of *Scheveningen* (at the Hague coast) *claims to be the largest herringfish harbor of all Europe.* A fact is, that for 300 years the Dutch herring held a monopoly on the European market. In the 16th and 17th centuries there were two thousand herringtubes (boats) and *one fifth of the entire Dutch population was occupied in the herring industry!* (450,000 men in those centuries according to Seafish guide by Elsevier, 1966, the whole population then being just over two million)

Think of that! One fifth! And think of all the other inhabitants of the Netherlands having such Zebulunitic occupations as ship building (very advanced for those days, even Czar Peter the Great from Russia came to learn ship building here!) draining, piling, making nets, building dykes, repairing harbors. It was Dutchmen who "sent to sea" — still a nostalgic dream of every Dutchman — who fought at sea, who traded at sea, who were pirates at sea, who were occupied with discovering foreign lands, like New Zealand. Think of the retired fishermen, the elderly men, who sit talking all day at the harbors! One may say that almost all the Dutch lived and worked, at least part of their days, at the seashore or natural harbors, fulfilling the blessing to Zebulun. The 16th — 19th centuries were the most blessed periods for Holland, being interna-tionally the heyday of fishing and shipping, when the expression made sense:

"Every Dutchman is a fisherman."

## FISHING ON "BOTH FLANKS"

Genesis 49 : 13 has sometimes been translated as "his borders

shall be unto Zidon," or as "at his flanks he shall catch fish."
(Ferrar Fenton) I remind you of the fact that both translations from
the Hebrew are correct on a different level. Here is a remarkable
example: Zidon is the name of a place in Palestine meaning "catching fish," nowadays it is identified with Saida, the fishing port
of the Lebanon. It is the end of the oil pipe-line of an Iraqi oil field
and the region has most eventful history, as the Canaanitish Sidon
was cursed with Tyre. (See Encyclopedia Britannica, nr 20, page 618,
1960 edition)

On a different level however "borders" become "thighs"
or flanks or sides, and Zidon meaning "catching fish," we suddenly
see with our inner eye a scene so common to those who know that
at least the Dutch fishermen mostly work in the Scheldt area and in
the Zuyderzee: A Dutch fisherboat having thrown his nets *on both
"flanks" of his boat* and balancing with its hull between the two
sides, is catching fish by dragging the nets over the sandy, often
shallow waters, maneuvring his boat through the deeper parts and
ever changing currents. This requires great skill and knowledge
passed on from father to son about the currents and tides. It is as
if we hear the Patriarch Zebulun repeating to his sons: "Observe
the waters and know when they flow together." Where else in the
world are the waters so "to be observed" or difficult to navigate but
so blessed with fish as in the clean (alas!) delta of the Rhine, the
Meuse and the Scheldt!

Where else but in the Netherlands is fishing from both sides so common? Where else is it so common to see the literal fulfillment of "Zebulun extending his legs to fishery" as in the Dutch shallow waters, where the fishermen with their leggings on walk up to their knees in the water to drag their nets in rain, wind or sunshine? Does the parallel still sound strange?

However we can translate the same Hebrew text on still another level, which, I must confess, is entirely my own, and I just lay it before you as seafood for thought and a vision, which I do pray will not materialise in its dramatic possibility. May my people collectively turn back from their selfmade Babylonic mess and close their doors for further psychic and physical dirt, pollution and sickness spreading like a cancer, whose name is none other than Baalzebul, before it is too late. May the Light, cleaning and purifying this blessed Delta's iniquities begin to shine here NOW, so that collectively we may shadow forth Israel, ruling with God.

## A VISION OF JACOB'S BLESSING TO ZEBULUN
## TURNED INTO A CURSE.

We have seen above that the word for ship is aniah in Hebrew, also meaning I or the self, and expecially in connection with lamenting, groaning. The human "I" laments for being incarnated in the flesh, longing for a lost paradise. The apostle Paul said all day long we are sighing over the creation.

Genesis 49:13, Jacob's blessing to Zebulun could be literally translated as:

"*Zebulun* (in the sense of those whose Lord is Zebul) *shall be caused to remain* (instead of freely dwell) *within dammed in* (embanked) *enclosures* (the word for hof) *of polluted waters,* (a dead seashore or dirty canals without life) *and the individual I's* (the "selves" as symbolic ships) *at these dammed* (in the double sᵒnse of the sound of the English word) *stagnant waters* (haven) *will be groaning and lamenting over the fish that are lying dead aside on their "flanks."*

The meaning of this translation could of course be interpreted entirely in a spiritual sense and be seen as the mental status of those who have dammed themselves in with psychic dirt and unclean thinking, so that the living inspiration (the fish) is dead, and only a stinking chaos of erotism and sick bodies are left. This could be the subject for a more psychological study. In the present book I'm trying to limit myself to showing the strange parallels on a national scale and on a level from which it can be visualised with the

47

outward eye.

Have you ever seen a school of poisoned fish in polluted water, showing their white flanks while floating in the dirty stinking water? Have you ever smelled them? If you have not, you may just as well imagine what is happening in the main Dutch rivers and canals and ditches and watery region all over the Netherlands. I take 1970, the European Conservation Year as the start of a period when the facts of our situation became available to the public, and action has now been taken to do something about it if not yet too late.

In the beginning of the 20th century the Rhine was still clear to the sandy bottom; the last salmon swam over the German border into the delta. It had no descendants, neither had the trout, nor so many other kinds of fish, which were Holland's treasure. If you refer to a fishing encyclopaedia, you may now cross out (yes, indeed with a cross, they have died in mass murder) almost all the varieties of fish found in the Netherlands. Only the strongest species still survive, and even those have often been poisoned and are dangerous to eat. The same applies to the Scheldt estuary.

This is no exaggeration. The Rhine is officially called the *sewer of Europe*.

Every Dutchman is now aware that the Netherlands are becoming the great sewer, the drain of Europe, united or not.

You remember the geography of the Netherlands, being blessed with international rivers? You can therefore easily imagine how all the poisoned and polluted waste water from the thousands of factories in France, Belgium, the Ruhr in Germany is drained off into the Rhine, the Meuse and the Scheldt. The lake of Constance in Switzerland, near which the Rhine has its source, is already too dirty to swim in, so you can imagine what kind of water after having passed German steel factories, to name just one kind, slowly flows into Holland, often artificially colored and rising in temperature. Until recently the Dutch drank this water!

Strange paradox, the most watery area of the world, the Dutch Delta, gets one of the biggest problems for future drinking water supplies for these thirteen million mouths on its hands. Everyone depends on water in the Netherlands, fishermen, farmers (cows drinking from a dirty ditch, so what about the milk, the butter, the cheese), and factories. The entire health situation, with every other house built at the water side depends on the famous traditional cleanliness, which is far to seek these days, when the "honor" of being the sewer of Europe is not always appreciated by the Dutch as a desired "service-task!"

The natural blessing of being the great
golden water-delta of Europe,
the natural blessing of having safe
harbors with still standing waters,
the blessing of being a nation, born and
bred at watersides,
the blessing of being a paradise for fish,
the blessing of being below sea level with
a comparatively mild climate,
seems to become a *curse*.
the unnatural curse of having to store the
dirt of the Europeans living nearer
the river head,
the unnatural curse of not getting rid of
pollution in stagnant waters,
the unnatural curse of dwelling on
stinking canals, not even being ad-
vised to swim in the polluted sea
along the dirty sandy coast,
the unnatural curse of being the mass
graveyard for water flora and
fauna,
the unnatural curse of low hanging clouds
with unbreathable air, descending
from all higher areas in Europe,
into the moist atmosphere of the
Low Lands, so that the days are
constantly dim and the light has
gone.

No blame rests on the other nations alone! The Dutch are wooing
their own fate too! Did you know that the ministry of public works,
the so-called Delta-project — which plans closing the sea-arms, the
natural tidal outlets — did result in shutting out the tides? This
means that the amount of pollution brought in by the great rivers
will no longer have a natural outlet into the sea. The sea ceases
functioning as a flush, while man-made chemical waste is being
accumulated in stagnant waters! Mad? The Delta-dykes were
planned in order to prevent future catastrophies like those of 1953.
However it is now realised by the best engineers that without
enormous expenditure on purifying installations it will lead to a
polluted catastrophy. But the building of the dykes goes on at full
speed, no matter what the Dutch have to sacrifice, because the
E.E.C. authorities wish to realize Rome's long cherished dream of a
direct overland motorway along the west coast of Europe to provide

a speedy connection with the projected Channel tunnel. A blessing or a curse? It is up to you to judge.

Is it too pessimistic a vision, based on facts, seeing the Dutch in the not too distant future as groaning and lamenting about live nature being killed? Even at this stage much has already been lost. It moves one to tears seeing the Dutch having to ''dwell'' with dirt, death and decay. It has always said, as a joke, that the *Dutch love grumbling,* because they never seem to be very grateful. The joke may acquire a sour taste. The Dutch these days are already losing their kind disposition and are becoming more irritated and start groaning. They are sulking like a spoiled child that is not given the asked for sweet.

The few individuals, the few ''I's'' who *see* in Holland, i.e. those who realise their identity with a tribe of *Israel,* those who still possess a conscious self in their heart, can do nothing but groan, lament and sigh. Unless they know their identity there is no solution. The only way out is getting faith in ''All Israel will be saved'' as prophesied in the Bible.

Only miracles can save us. One should be *prepared to be cleansed and to make sacrifices for the right causes.* Miracles will be performed when Holland's blindness is cured. If the strange parallel is a true parallel, then literally Israel will dwell alone and safely in the catastrophic days to come.

May Holland be cleansed and clean again, may there be light instead of darkness in the Lowlands, and may the return of the Light be seen here first, as at His first appearance in Zebulun's land. (Matthew 4:13-15)

# CHAPTER 7.

## HOLLAND A HAVEN FOR THE PERSECUTED

A happier translation of Jacob's blessing than the foregoing may be seen even as a vision for the future, but it certainly has a strange parallel in the past:

*"Holland a haven for philosophers."*

This is a quotation of Chapter nine in Charles Wilson's excellent book on the Dutch Republic in the 17th century!

Note: this is not the 19th century *John* Wilson from Cambridge, we are quoting *Charles* Wilson, now lecturer in modern history also at Cambridge.

Professor Charles Wilson devotes a chapter on *the religious persecuted* from many countries in those days, who found refuge in the Netherlands:

"By far the largest group were Flemings or Walloons from the south, but they were far from being the only prominent newcomers. They were joined by Germans, Scandinavians, French, English, Scots, Jews, even Armenians, Turks. The large towns were cosmopolitan to an extent *unique in the seventeenth century world...* Almost all *foreign immigrants came in search for freedom from persecution*, whether they were great merchants from Antwerp, skilled textile workers from Ypres, or scholars from France or England."

> *Charles Wilson in the Dutch Republic, page 165, World University Library, London, 1968.*

Among these scholars were Rene *Descartes*, Baruch de *Spinoza*, John *Locke*, to name only a few. Many were *Huguenots* who after the edict of Nantes flocked in thousands to the Protestant Netherlands. Many a Dutchman can still claim descendency from them.

The famous *Mayflower-group* who sailed for America in 1620, first settled in Amsterdam and Leyden under their pastor John Robinson. They found protection in the Netherlands for many years.

Spinoza was a Jew. *Holland always has been a "haven" for Jews.* In the 15th and 16th centuries thousands of *Sephardic* Jews fled from Spain towards the Netherlands, mainly settling in *Amsterdam,* which until the second world war was still called "Mokum" (which means good place) or the "Jerusalem of the North." Names like Cohen, de Levita, Jessurun, de Pinto are well known and respected in Amsterdam. They have enriched the Dutch culture for many ages. Their skill at silver work, diamond-cutting, medicine, music, Hebrew, was outstanding and could grow in peace in Holland. When the Bible was translated around 1620, Dutch theologians were greatly assisted by Sephardic Jews. Rembrandt painted them as Biblical illustrations.

In later ages Ashkenazim Jews escaping from their fate in Russia, Poland and Germany also found refuge in the Netherlands. During all these ages *Jews never lived in ghetto's* in Holland, the only country in Europe where they were not discriminated against.

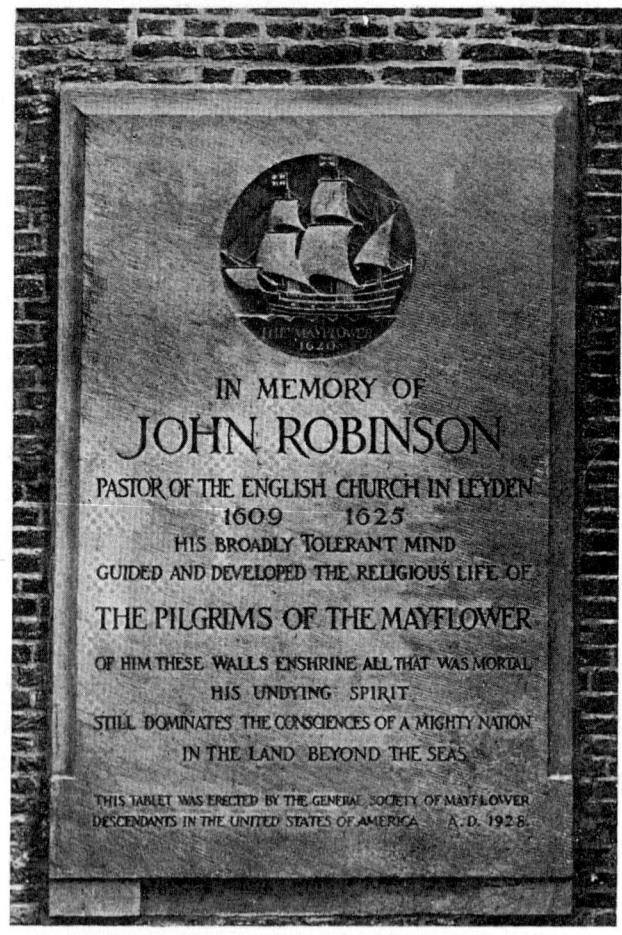

PLAQUE IN PIETERSCHURCH AT LEYDEN

# CHAPTER 8.

## THE HEBREW WORD FOR HAVEN IDENTICAL WITH HOLLAND'S HOF

It was the Rev. John Wilson a hundred and fifty years ago, who made the remark in his book on our Israelitish Origin, that the Hebrew word "chof," meaning haven, sounds the same as the Dutch word hof, having the same meaning. He probably was nearer the mark than he himself knew. Anyhow following this line we come to some remarkable parallels.

(Note: a series of articles on this subject was written in Een Nieuw Geluid, Oct. 1967 - Feb. 1968 by the authoress)

In the dialects of Zealand and Flanders, *the g and ch are interchangeable with the h.* The same occurs in Hebrew and Gaelic. For instance an old Zealand farmer in his traditional black national costume with golden filigrane buttons on his collar, when inviting you to visit his farm, will tell you "kom op't chof." This literally means "come within the gates of my property."

The word "chof" for haven, meaning originally "an enclosure" also expresses exactly what the Dutch word "hof" is and means: an enclosure with a fence, or surrounded by pile and twined reeds.

*Etymologically speaking the Dutch word Hof is one of the oldest words existing in this language and one with the most varied meanings within the conception of an enclosure!*

Here are a few examples of everyday usages of the Dutch word "hof:"

1) the oldest hof are the *Houses of Parliament* in The Hague, *The Binnenhof.* (Origin in the 7th century) Originally the Dukes had their hof-days there. The Governmental buildings are built *in a square* around an open court, with the main building almost in the centre, thus forming the enclosure.

2) The *Residence of the Royal Family* is called "Hof." Those who are serving the Queen are the "Hofhouding." (Hof-holding)

3) A large, typical *Dutch farm* with all her separate buildings and garden around, often fenced in with a ditch or a row of trees, is a "HOF."

4) The *Dutch Courts* with judges are officially called "het Hof."

5) A beautifully kept *enclosed garden* is called a "hof." Internationally known is "Keukenhof," where thousands of tourists admire the flowers in the spring. (illustration nr. 9)

6) The *garden of Eden* in the Dutch Bible is called "Hof van Eden"

7) An old-fashioned word for *courting a girl* is "hof-maken." (the man is asking the girl to make his "hof," to be his haven)

53

The Houses of Parliament

8) The *almshouses* (which they are not!) or ancient communities of single ladies, one person dwellings built in a square, are of a typical Dutch origin. Nowadays they are historical gems and a combination of Israel's care for its widows and being an example of a typically Dutch "haven" or "hof," Let us have a closer look at them:

## DUTCH HOFJES, A MARK OF ZEBULUN?

The idea "Hofje" had its origin in the Netherlands in about the 13th century. They were first built in Flanders for elderly women (often rich, so that it is not right to compare them with an almshouse), not to be confused with nunneries, although in Belgium they sometimes have been taken over by the Roman Catholic Church. In Holland the idea "Hofje" was entirely identified with the Protestant culture, and it reminds us of the enclosures and safe haven of Zebulun, for the principle was to have settlements of houses, for single persons built in a square around the pump and garden with gatehouse as entrance to the street, where single women could live a free, independent and safe life.

The principle behind it was the Mosaic law to care for the orphans and the widows and it was "done" in the 16th-17th centuries by the Calvinistic nobility and rich merchants. They got their fortunes through their overseas trade to finance a Hofje to which they either gave their own name for posterity or a Biblical one. So we still have architectural gems with names like: Bethlehem-Hofje, Sions-Hofje, Holy Ghost-Hofje. It is certainly a Dutch dwelling invention, though later on copied by other countries, especially Denmark. There are still about one hundred and fifty larger and smaller Hofjes left in the Netherlands, either still inhabited by single women or again serving as a modern form of refuge, this time to escape modern traffic noises and impersonal glass and steel apartment blocks. Nowadays they are often inhabited by artists and students. A modern haven for creative work.

## THE NETHERLANDS A COUNTRY OF HAVEN WITH THE WORLD'S LARGEST HARBOR

Unless you have criss-crossed the small Netherlands many times, you will never realise how without exaggeration almost every town or village is situated by the water edge, which has functioned as a natural harbor. Look at the map of the Netherlands: The islands in the south-west, where all the villages are built along these sea-arms; the long coast of Holland, harbors with natural seaside resorts. Look at the coast bending inland forming the Zuyderzee, now closed by a dam, but still bordered by innumerable

ROTTERDAM PORT.

pretty ancient little towns and villages, where life is centred around the harbors. Now take Friesland in the north, full of shallow still safe pools and lakes strewn about their flat meadows.

However this is not yet the end of the number of Netherland's natural harbors: The three great rivers, Rhine, Meuse, Scheldt with their slow moving waters are being bordered almost every other kilometer by a village with some shipyards. Apart from the big ones, there are innumerable smaller rivers, mostly canalised, along which the Dutch built quays with houses.

Truly, where else in the world does a people exist, blessed so systematically with flat watery land, and where in the world have the homes alongside the "haven" a more characteristic parallel with Zebulun, than in the innumerable little port-towns of Holland?

## ROTTERDAM, LARGEST WORLD PORT

Speaking about haven in the modern sense, is it so strange that small Holland has the largest port in the world within its borders, namely Rotterdam-Europoort? It has surpassed London, New York and Hamburg. Willy nilly it is becoming the premier port of the European Community. The name itself, Europoort is the Dutch abbreviated word for "gate of Europe." It is too far fetched to remind you that Israel, living in the Isles of the West, will possess the (sea) gates of their enemies, as prophesied in Genesis 22:17; 24:60. Incidentally, as far as our comparison with Zebulun is concerned it is a nice little touch that Rotterdam-Europoort has as its modern symbol a large watch-tower called Euro-mast, like the mast of a ship.

At Rotterdam the international rivers Rhine and Meuse become confluent. According to ancient legend it was Ratherius in 90 A.D. who founded Rotterdam, being a descendant of the Royal Trojans, who again claimed to belong to the tribe of Judah. (see Rev. W.M.H. Milner's The Royal House of Britain an enduring dynasty, 13th edition 1964, Covenant Books, London)

## RECAPITULATION, OF CHAPTERS FOUR TO EIGHT:

We have been dealing with the blessings of Jacob to his son Zebulun given in Genesis 49:13, which prophesied about the status of the tribe, as dwelling at the haven, being blessed with a fishing fleet, and the way he will be fishing.

Parallels have been shown with the geographical position of the Netherlands, their natural harbors, the way the Dutch are living and "dwelling" and their art of architecture has been demonstrated.

Examples have been given of the Dutch word "hof," which is Hebrew for haven. The symbol for Zebulun and Dutch ships has been compared. The importance of herring and other fish in the Netherlands have been stressed. A vision of a future curse has been given, which will become a fact if the Dutch don't quickly purify their own waters. The typical methods of Dutch fishing as an example of the Hebrew words has been demonstrated. The Dutch mentality of welcoming every foreigner who is persecuted and Holland as a haven for writers have been mentioned. Even the ghostly world of the Flying Dutchman has been brought to the forefront as an eerie parallel with Zebulun's ships.

Chapter nine will now give a brief parallel with the tradition of the Patriarch.

Chapter ten is devoted to the activities of Zebulun as prophesied by Moses and the strange parallel with the Dutch suckers and milkers.

Chapter eleven speaks about Zebulun's talents with the pen and Holland's advanced talent for printing and bookreading, as well as laying claim to the invention of the art of printing.

# CHAPTER 9.

## ZEBULUN'S COMPASSION FOR THE UNDERDOG

These are not Biblical words. However based on ancient Jewish tradition, it may teach us something about Zebulun's mentality handed down through the ages.

Greatly stressed is his image as the most compassionate one of the twelve children of Israel.

He had compassion on his brother Joseph. Hence, he commands his descendants to have mercy upon their neighbours, "to have compassion towards all, not towards men only, but also towards beasts. Have compassion in your hearts, because when my brethren were sickening and dying on account of Joseph, because they showed no mercy in their hearts, my sons were preserved without sickness as you know," reads the Testament of the Patriarch. Zebulun saw a man in distress, being naked, and he had compassion upon him and secretly stole away a garment from his father's house, and gave it to him who was in distress. "Do ye therefore my children, from that which God bestoweth upon you, *show compassion and mercy without hesitation to all men and give to every man with a good heart*...I know that my hand found not the wherewithal to give him that needed, and I walked with him weeping for seven furlongs, and my bowels yearned towards him in compassion."

## THE DUTCH COMPASSION ON THE UNDERDOG

In every century individual Dutchmen dealing with Spaniards, Indians, Africans, were as far removed from Christian love as any other wild white western Anglo-Saxon, but at home and as a nation they are throughout history known as a compassionate and peaceful people. They are indeed *renowned for their compassion on those in need.* The care for the sick, the poor, disabled, the mentally disturbed has always been an example to other nations. Being a homely people, neighbourly help has always been the inner strength of the nation, and in times when the cities of the western world started demolishing their slums, Holland had hardly any.

However Holland's mentality of compassion can easily degenerate in Holland into sheer busy-bodiness, which nowadays may lead to hysterics in the overpopulated country. Shown on a national scale it can sometimes become ridiculous. Everybody is minding everybody else's business. And when little Holland is going to tell other nations how to handle their internal affairs, it becomes meddlesomeness. This is far removed from "walking with the other weeping for seven furlongs," which undoubtedly is the mental attitude of the best of our Dutch leaders, led by the Dutch Royal Family.

Anyhow it is a fact that the spontaneity with which the population of the Netherlands responds to calls for the charity beats all other countries. A national collection for disasters in other countries like food for India, earthquakes in Persia, children in Biafra gather enormous sums. These do not come from a few rich millionaires. They come from the average man, woman and child in the street all over the Netherlands.

Becoming emotional about the underdog in the world seems to be the peculiar mentality exclusively to the Anglo-Saxon-Celtic people (which includes the Scandinavians)—a mark in itself of Israel—but only the Dutch go so far in their compassion that they are getting very emotional about it. The closing stages of a national collection are assuming epidemic proportions. The mass-media play upon the emotions of the Dutch; many are glued to their T.V. sets on such a day of a national ingathering to see how much is coming in minute by minute from this town, or that factory or such a school or apartments-flat. From ships and churches they all send messages and money to the national collecting centre. However hysterical as it sometimes may become, it is a truly *national example, which is unique in the world.* It shows a strange parallel with the words of Zebulun to his descendants.

The reverse of this medal is that the Dutch on the whole are too indiscriminate as to where the distribution of the money goes, and when found out, the grumbling, that other peculiar national trait, comes later! It can become dangerous too in these days when a few through the mass media can play on the emotions of the Dutch in their homes and make them dip into their pockets for any dubious political aim. Blindly they drive their bent for compassion too far and like Israel of old they get a rude awakening when the Canaanites, whom they had bred, stood up against them within their own gates.

Could the reverse of Zebulun's command be a blind exaggeration of the Dutch passion for compassion on the underdeveloped underdog, and ought not they sometimes lock their doors against them in the future and behind themselves with more Israelitic discrimination?

In former days Holland was blessed, being a refuge for foreigners and their compassion was a positive thing. Nowadays the free immigration of foreign laborers with their different morals has become a problem (a curse) to the Netherlands. It is causing psychic pollution by too much busi-bodiness with these adverse elements. Being part of Real Israel the Dutch have to cleanse their own house. Look in the mirror: Zebulun did not drive out the Canaanites from Kithron and Nahallel as ordered in Deutronomy 7 and mentioned in Judges 1:7.

## ZEBULUN'S CITIES OF NAHALLEL AND NEHALENNIA.

I have not gone into the meaning of all the names of places given to Zebulun by lot. This is too specialized a subject for this book. I want to make one exception: *Zebulun has twelve cities. One of them in the North is called Nahallel, meaning green pastures.* It is said that the Zebulunites did not drive out the heathen inhabitants of Nahallel.

In 1647 there was found a temple of a heathen goddess on the island of Walcheren at the Scheldt with the name inscribed in stone *Nehalennia.* Immediately after these findings there were Dutch and English theologians of those days tracing her name back to... Nahal, meaning pasture, suggesting she was derived from the Scythian language.

ALTARSTONES DEDICATED TO NEHALENNIA (A GUARDIAN OF THE SEAFARERS)

61

NEDERLAND-ZEBULUN
parallel in postzegels

62

# CHAPTER 10

## MOSES' BLESSING TO ZEBULUN: SUCK THE SEAS

Moses, Israel's great leader, standing before the Promised Land, sings about Zebulun's future:

"Rejoice Zebulun in thy going out. They shall call the people to the mountain, there they shall offer sacrifices of righteousness. They shall suck of the abundance of the sea and of the treasures hid in the sand."

(In the Book of Laws for Israel, Deuterononmy 33:18-19)

The end of this song is most illuminating. Again we may translate the Hebrew words on different levels and every time one may discover striking "strange parallels" with the image of little Holland in the world, an image greatly exploited by Dutch advertisements for attracting tourists into the country.

*Unconciously the Dutch tourist-offices are advertising exactly what Zebulun had prophesied he would be doing and exporting*:! reclaiming land, putting fingers in dykes, living in windmills sucking water, and all the Dutch being shown as blond cheese-heads milking their Friesian cows or making cheese and butter in some fancy national costume, everybody with smiling faces, rejoicing, with Dutch tulips in their hands good for export. Yes indeed, modern export propaganda and exploitation of past Dutch folk-lore still shows in a mirror a strange parallel with Zebulun!

## THE DUTCH ARE "SUCKERS" AND "MILKERS."

Yes, they certainly are, in more than one sense! Let us look from a humourous angle how others see us and how our character is being reflected in water and milk, both so abundant in Holland!

You would laugh at the numerous composite words and expressions including the word "milk" in a Dutch dictionary! The most spectacular one is "melkmuil" (milk-mouth) meaning greenhorn, or is it...a sucker?! Pardon this pun, but the point is, that in Hebrew we read literally:

*"They shall milk* (therefore translated as "suck") *the abundance of the waters."* This word for milking can mean both giving milk and suckling milk.

The verse of Moses has sometimes been interpreted as: Israel having to dig for treasures in the sea like oil, amber, uranium. Although probably not being untrue, there are other texts in the Bible concerning other tribes referring to oil, which is beyond the scope of our subject. It is far more to the point to take the meaning of the text as it stands:

*Sucking the surplus of (sea) water and delving up the sand itself.*

The sand in itself is already a treasure, because new dykes, new land is being made out of it. The latter will become pasture with grazing cows. These are the true Dutch treasures:

*the reclaimed fat land of sand and mud giving treasures of milk and cheese,* which yielded easy riches to the farmers in their golden days of free enterprise. (Not suggesting that a farmer is not a hard worker, but it is nature, reclaimed nature, which gives the Netherlands its wealth)

## THE DUTCH DISCOVERED THE "GAS BELL."

Northsea-gas, which is becoming very popular in western Europe, has been discovered by Dutch engineers. In 1962 they discovered a huge "gas bell" under the northern Netherlands and the North sea, while boring for oil! Sucking gas in abundances from the seas! What a treasure for the Celtic fringe this new gas-belt has become!

## SUCKING THE WATER BY A WINDMILL
## THROUGH THE POWER OF THE WIND.

What is more Dutch than the sight of a working windmill in a flat green Dutch landscape? Although those who have studied the history of the windmills, have traced them back to Medo-Persia—you remember Zebulun as one of the ten tribes which was deported to that area—the Dutch have refined the buildings and engineering of windmilling at least from as far back as 1200 A.D. *The invention of the waterwindmill for drainage purposes, with the screw action lifting or "hooking" the water from a lower to a higher level is exclusively Dutch.*

Apart from this, the variety of windmills in the Netherlands is greater than anywhere else in the world. On the power of the wind their age-old wooden engines worked as flour, spicery and oil grinders, as sawmills, as papermakers, as printing presses, as gin-distillers. In the golden 17th century the Netherlands had thousands of turning windmills with the always blowing westwind sucking and sighing harder through its wings, making the wheels go turning harder and more efficient, than many a modern machine after the invention of electricity.

This is not meant as a plea for a return to a former century. It is *just a drawing of strange parallels between the blessings to Zebulun and the essentials of Dutch historical culture and achievements in historical times,* although it was indeed a more blessed period for Holland's peace of mind when men worked in harmony with the natural powers of nature. The Netherlands were an organic unity, independent and self - supporting when using the powers of nature only. They could indeed rejoice in their going out, as Moses sang, in their large wooden ships, whose planks had been cut by the power of the windmills, and rejoice when returning with these ships laden with Eastern spices to be ground by the power of the mills. No manpower was needed but for one miller who was skilled in wind-and weather-forecast in order to set the sails of his "factory" to the wind in God's right time. Imagine how one miller during a strong wind can handle an ordinary mill with huge sails (twenty-seven meter, 81 feet, across the height of the mill once as much again). These man-made treasures kept the land dry by drainage, while the cows graze it. Sucking, milking.

In recent times, when the power of electricity was cut off during the second world war, the mills were freely used again, and nowadays about 1000 have been restored, many of them still working, because windmilling for which one has to pass an exam is becoming a favorite hobby of young Dutchmen.

## "GOD CREATED THE WORLD,
## BUT THE DUTCH CREATED HOLLAND."

*"God created the world, but the Dutch created Holland"* is an old Dutch saying. Anyhow Dutch engineers have been asked for advice in drainage-projects throughout the ages.

Prof. Ch. *Wilson* devoted a chapter (page 80-91) in his book *"The Dutch Republic"* to the areas the Dutch reclaimed in Western Europe and England from the 13th to the 17th centuries. For instance the Royal Park at Windsor, the Lincoln and Cambridge Fens, parts of Kent, Somerset, East Anglia, but also parts of France, Italy and Germany.

The Dutch know how to grow crops on reclaimed land and how to remove excess salt.
"At the same time," according to Wilson, "the famous breed of *Friesian cattle* was making its appearance in Britain. Mortimer, writing in 1707, remarked that the long-legged short-horned cow of the Dutch breed found in Lincolnshire and Kent was the best breed for milking."

"Rejoicing in their going out," many descendants of these Dutch-Friesian cows nowadays block the roads to hasty motorists, who are driving their cars through the winding roads of Somerset.

## DUTCH EMIGRANTS, REJOICING THEIR GOING OUT!

Dutch export of cheese and butter, but also Dutch export of engineers, of farmers and of intellectuals is flourishing. Do you know that compared with other countries the Dutch send out the largest percentage of the population to farm and to teach farming in the West and nowadays also in under-developed countries?

Did you know that only 50 out of 500,000 Dutch emigrants don't suceed and need help or return? This is an extremely low percentage, according to the Netherlands Emigration Service. (Elsevier's magazine, June 1971) Moreover Dutch immigrants often seem to have stable families and can easily adapt themselves to their new environments. Another parallel with Zebulun's "rejoicing in their going out?"

## DUTCH MISSIONARIES

This going out can also be translated as "going abroad" and when the text speaks of Zebulun calling the people to the mountain, which is often seen as a symbol for Jerusalem, it is not too far fetched to compare this with the Dutch Protestant and Roman Catholic Missions. Next to Great Britain and the United States the Netherlands have the honor to have been the third missionary nation, their main fields of activity having been Indonesia, their former colonies (84 million inhabitants in 1960). Although the mission has had its hey-day, one cannot underestimate the Calvinistic (mostly Dutch-Reformed) principles that have been spread around the globe. Neither should the Mennonites, Methodist- and Presbyterian groups, having their roots in the Netherlands, which settles in the United States and grew into astronomical numbers, been forgotten, when thinking of Zebulun "rejoicing in his going out." New York was founded by the Dutch as "New Amsterdam."

## SOUTH AFRICA A DUTCH PLANTATION

Neither can any historian ever deny that South Africa is mainly a Dutch plantation. The interests of the Duth East India Company with their speedy "flyboats" in the 17th century were mixed with the missionary activities of the young Protestant Republic in the 16th and 17th centuries with its many refugees, mainly Huguenots, who have formed the bulk of the Dutch settlers in South Africa. Undoubtedly their going out has become a blessing for that land. Is it still

strange that there are groups in South Africa today who see themselves as offshoots of Zebulun through their descendency from
Holland?

## OFFERING SACRIFICES OF RIGHTEOUSNESS

This being a difficult text in itself, I have not yet received the
inspiration for the determination of a satisfying parallel with Holland, unless one might see this as prospective a task for the purpose
of calling the nations to Jerusalem, centre of the world, by being
able to speak many languages,(the average Dutchman learns four
languages) where the Dutch and their offshoots, the South-Africans
will be offering sacrifices of righteousness in the sense of being
politically seen as black-sheep by their keeping, as a nation, to the
letter of the Bible. They will have to sacrifice a lot for this righteousness in the near future. In this respect both the Dutch and the South
Africans have a high calling amongst the nations. This is only one
interpretation. There are certainly more.

## THE DUTCH SPLITTING UP INTO MANY STREAMS

Instead of calling to one spiritual mountain, they are often too
divided among themselves. As the Patriarch said in his Testament,
the Dutch especially, as his descendents are too much split up into
little parties and opinions, so that they are not one unit of force.
*"Unity makes force"* (Union is strength) *was the official device of
the Republic of the Netherlands when fighting Spain,* but in the past
they have often been too weak to make their cry heard internationally
or to awaken the right spirit in other peoples. This is how Zebulun
warned his children:

"If you are divided into many streams, the earth swalloweth
them up and they become of no account. So shall ye also be if ye
be divided. Be not ye therefore divided into two heads, for
everything the Lord has made has but one head···"(IX 2-4)

Revealing are such expressions about Dutchmen as: "Three
Dutchmen, three different churches." "Wherever two Dutchmen
meet in a pub, they start a theological row." "So many men, so
many minds."

Nowhere in the western world have there been so many split-
ups in churches and political parties as in the Netherlands. Nowhere
exist so much hair-splitting and quibbling about internal political
details considering what is going on in the world at large. Did the
Patriarch forsee this splitting up by the Dutch?

Anyhow the best remedy against mental division always has

been the physical *joined struggle against the water*. In their great projects of impoldering, making dykes and defending their country against floods and disasters, the best traits of the Dutch national character come to the surface. In fighting a common enemy, the Dutch have more than once proven to be *no small nation at heart*.

## NOT OF DOUBLE HEART

Leaving Moses' blessing now I'm referring here in passing to the 50,000 *zebulunites* in the Bible, who are said to be *"not of double heart"*. In other words: *A courageous and reliable people!* They came to fight at King David's side. He could rely on these Zebulunites. (I Chron. 12 : 33). The allies could rely on the Dutch in the last world war. May it be the same in the future!

# CHAPTER 11.

## DEBORAH'S BLESSING TO ZEBULUN: WIELDING THE PEN OF THE WRITER

This time a woman, being a judge in Israel, is singing her prophecy regarding the children of Zebulun, now being free and at home in their Promised Land. The Zebulunites had received a portion of the land by lot and they had taken an active part in the fight to sweep the country and to throw off the tyranny of Jabin the Canaanite, for which battle Deborah, the woman judge, had summoned 10,000 Zebulunites of whom she now says:

*"Zebulun's men risked their lives to death."* (Judges 5 : 18)
and "Come to me with *Zebulun wielding the writer's pen.*"

(Judges 5 : 14).

This means handling the pen of the writer, or skilled in writing. It sometimes has been translated as *"the recruitersstaff,"* which means a military call. On this different level it has the same function: by writing or by recruiting one is calling others to mental or physical action and jointly to enlist or to enroll into something. That is the function of this present book as well!: recruiting a small Gideon's band of people who will stand for real Israel.

However these Hebrew words still have another meaning. The "pen" is here literally *"branched off stick or scion for punishing,"* (Strong Concordance) for writing, for fighting, for ruling.

It was especially used in this sense to inscribe, to recount, to number. The word used here is "sepher," which is known in the Bible as the word for a book or a roll.

It is therefore not out of place to associate it with the means for producing books and printing letters.

## THE DUTCH CLAIM THE INVENTION OF THE PRINTED WORD.

Prior to the Middle Ages the Lowlands were already renowned for their beautifully calligraphed breviaries on parchment.

What became the means for producing books since the 14th century? Small "branched off" sticks of lead and molds of letters! Movable letters of tin and lead, still used by printer nowadays. Do you realise what a far reaching and revolutionary invention it has been to obtain the *means for duplicating books?!*

Who would be the first to get this brilliant idea which was going to revolutionise the intellectual mind? It would lead up *the freedom of the printed word* and availability of the Bible to the average citizen.

Zebulun was to be blessed with the skill of numbering "branched off" sticks or letters. Here is the strange parallel:

The Dutch claim to have invented this!

For ages this has been a hot historical question, and it is still generally accepted in the Anglo-Saxon world that it was a German, Gutenberg, who invented the printing press. The Dutch have always disputed this on good grounds, and recent discoveries in Germany give even more credit to the Dutch claim!

## LAURENS JANSZOON COSTER OF HAARLEM

Here is the Dutch story behind it, which by the way, millions of Dutch have been taught at school to be the truth!

In the city of Haarlem there is a statue in the market-place of a man with a letterblock in his hand. On the stone is inscribed: 1440 A.D. "Typographiae letteris mobilibus a metallo fusis inventor," or the inventor of the art of printing with movable letters, of cast metal.

Coster having invented this primitive way of printing with lead types was robbed of his invention on Christmas night of 1440 A.D. by his servant Jan, who fled with it to Mainz in Germany, where it eventually came into the hands of Gutenberg, who seems to have refined the method and produced the famous Gutenberg-Bible in 1448. After a centuries old tug of war between the Dutch and Germans (there is a vast literature pro and contra) a conclusion seems to have been reached recently, since a 15th century Chronicle has been rediscovered in Cologne (Germany) mentioning that before Gutenberg, prints were already made in Holland. Moreover as a result of research there is evidence that astronomical calenders in Mainz exist, printed in a more primitive style than Gutenberg's. Are these examples servant Jan brought with him? Anyhow Coster printed such astronomical calenders in Haarlem in Gutenberg's time.

See in Dutch (Modern Encyclopedia of World Literature, Seven Volumes in Dutch) under Coster. In English the Encyclopaedia Britannica (vol. II and vol. 18, 1961 edition) under the heading "printing" still names Gutenberg "the strongest claimant to the honor of the invention of printing" and "because Laurens Coster of Haarlem (Holland) is the only man whose name can be connected with these prints, (whose work is much more primitive than that of Gutenburg and therefore assumedly preceded this) *he is considered by some scholars the first inventor of printing.*"

## DUTCH PRINTING AND CALLIGRAPHY OUTSTANDING

Whatever is the historical truth about this invention, it remains a fact that the Dutch were and still are world-famous for "handling the pen of the writer" as calligraphers, often drawing in one line.

The illustrations show two examples by Jan van de Velde Sr., a 17th century Dutch painter, famous for his painting of ships. Two of his best calligraphed drawings are by chance (!) showing us the strange Parallel between Zebulun and the Dutch:

A hand, wielding the writers pen, Deborah's blessing; and the symbol of the ship, which is Zebulun's banner. The present Dutch calligraphers still enjoy international fame for their drawing of charters.

In the international printers-language many words and names of *letters are of Dutch origin*   Many a printer outside the Netherlands will hardly know nowadays that he is daily using a Lowlanders name Christoffel *Plantin,* (letter type) *the great industrial printer* of the Netherlands (Leyden and Antwerp) in the 16th century, the printer to Royalty, politicians and scientists of those days.

Dutch printing and bookbinding is a most interesting and important subject, but as it is too vast in itself, I have to suffice here with mentioning a few examples to demonstrate that especially the *Netherlands have always been advanced and blessed in the arts of writing and printing.*   If anywhere in the western world, the "epitheton ornans," given by the prophetess to Zebulun, became true, it would be in the Lowlands: They deserve the honored title of "recruiters by means of the pen."

### HOLLAND HAS ALWAYS BEEN A HAVEN
### FOR THE FREEDOM OF THE PRINTED WORD.

Where refugees in the 16th-17th century could freely print their religious ideas? Don't we have a remarkable combination here of Jacob's blessing to Zebulun, of being a haven, and Moses' words of "being blessed in thy going out with joy" (think of all the Dutch

73

Der schrijver's pen.
(J. van de Velde de Oude, Spieghel der Schrijfkonste, 1605)

74

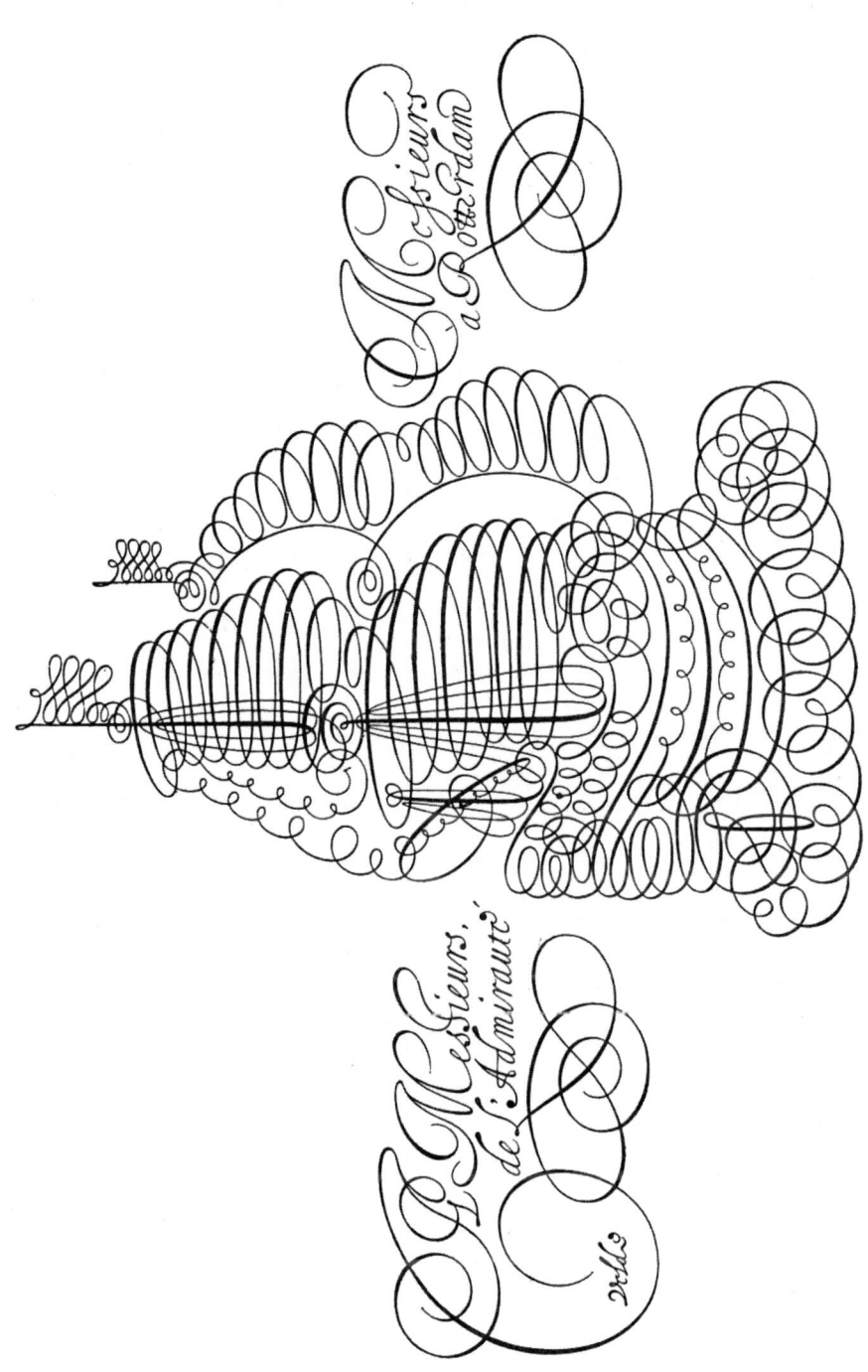

books having gone the world over!) and Deborah's prophecy that Zebulun's talent for the "sepher," the book, will be blessed?

The Dutch have been and still are greatly blessed in finding new methods of printing. From the 15th-18th centuries they were the leading nation. From the Encyclopaedia Britannica I quote, (vol 18, 1960 Edition) "Even England was completely dependant for type on the Dutch."

Recently *Dutch color-printing* and the latest methods of *phototype* have been developed in the Netherlands. Orders for the highest quality of art-printing from all over the world are being placed by the United States and Great Britain as well. This again is drawing a far-sighted parallel with the light-prophecy for Zebulun mentioned in Chapter twelve.

## DUTCH EXCELL IN CARTOGRAPHY,
## A REMINISCENCE OF ZEBULUN?

The Dutch have always excelled in cartography and making maps for navigation-purposes. "In the following (17th) century in the production of high-grade maps the Dutch were supreme, as is illustrated by classic atlases of Mercator, W.J. and J. Blaeu, H. Hondius, J. Janssen and N. Visscher," writes Encyclopaedia Britannica, (vol. 2, 1960 Edition under atlas) and, by 1600 Amsterdam had succeeded Antwerp as the center of cartographic industry in the Netherlands, and the 17th century was the great age of Dutch map production. ''(idem mr. 14, under map) Flemish cartographers gave the first impetus to the art of map engraving in England.

The very *first sea atlas, Spieghel der Zeevaerdt* (Mirror of Navigation) was both made and printed in the Netherlands in 1584, followed by many more by means of which the sailors of those days could beat the Spaniards and were better equipped to sail the seven seas.

THE DUTCH EXCELL IN CARTOGRAPHY EVEN IN THE HEAVENS
(MIDDLEBURG 17TH CENTURY)

Do you now realise that Dutch history is plainly showing us our strange parallel with Zebulun? It is so simple that I greatly wonder why nobody saw it before. Do we have to be blind?!

Here again three words by Zebulun have been combined:
The old dying man said to his sons ''observe the waters and know when they flow together.'' What else is cartography of the sea than

77

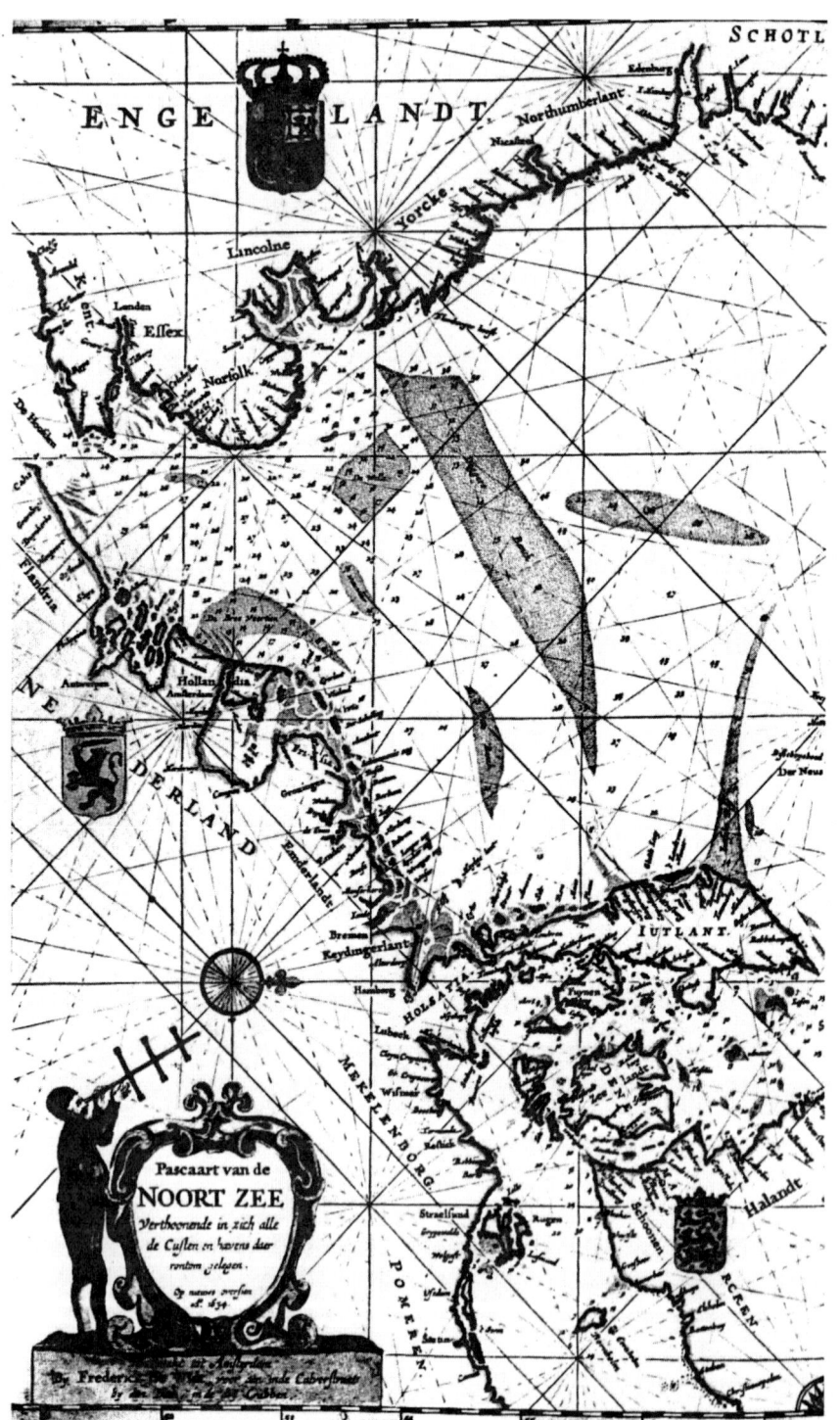

doing it by "handling the pen of the writer," this being Zebulun's future? Combine this again with Moses' words of "rejoicing in thy going out." Isn't it strange that especially the Dutch have been greatly blessed by printing navigation maps for those who rejoice going out to sea?

Not only maps, but also the sea laws concerning the boundaries of the seas apportioned to the nations have been "invented" by Hugo Grotius in the beginning of the 17th century. This Dutch lawyer and his books printed three centuries ago are still the basis of the rules of international territorial waters.

## DUTCH EXCELL IN HYDROGRAPHY, THE PATRIARCH ZEBULUN'S VISION.

Nowhere in the world the currents and streams and sandbanks are apt to change due to the tides so much so as in the Netherlands. The Dutch always excelled in hydrography, which means description of the waters of the earth. In our days there is a Dutch export of brains in the form of Delft's hydrographical and hydroolgical engineers who are the world's best.

## CENTRAL POSITION OF THE BOOK IN DUTCH HOMES.

Books and the printed word in general are a living reality for the average Dutchman. Almost in every Dutch home one may find at least a few books on a shelf, which are really read (apart from having books as token to keep up with the "Jansens!") and indeed a recent survey of rough statistics gives the Netherlands by far the highest quota of readers: 60% against for instance 20% in the United States. These figures don't say too much as they do not reveal the quality of the reading. However it is true to say that the Dutch share with the Swiss the ability *to read in four languages*. (Dutch, English, French, German are taught in all secondary schools)

Not only reading, but also writing is a part-time hobby. The quality and quantity of writers in Dutch (embracing Flanders,

Belgium and South Africa, as well as the Dutch emigrants all over the world, being all together about 20 million) is extremely high, but very underestimated in other countries because of the language-barrier.

## HANDLING THE PEN OF THE WRITER FOR SAINT NICOLAAS.

This is just a joke. However, where in the world can such a crazy old popular custom be found as in the Netherlands on the 5th of December, when suddenly every Dutchman becomes a poet and is giving presents accompanied by humorous or satyrical nonsense in verse or by a long poem making fun of the one who is at the receiving end? All this anonymous writing by millions and treated as coming from the Saint (no Santa Claus!) is a very broad "handling the pen of the writer!"

Things can be expressed very accurately in Holland and one of our 17th century Dutch classic writers (Vondel) is still cited: "Het gouden puntje van de pen is 't felste wapen dat ik ken." *The golden point of the pen is the fiercest weapon I know.*

### THE WRITERS' PEN A BLESSING,
### A CURSE WHEN MIS—RECRUITED.

As with the other blessings, the people can turn them into a self-willed curse if they shy away from the cosmic laws of God laid down for Israel. Recruiting and punishing with the pen was a blessing for Zebulun *within* the Promised Land.

What do we see nowadays especially in Holland? The Netherlands, always having been a buffer-state, now seems to become *an ideological battlefield* of the freedom of the printed word. They seem to become a melting pot of international filth. What can't be done yet in other countries, is floating freely towards the Netherlands as the psychic and symbolic counterpart of the polluted waters of the river Rhine, Meuse and Scheldt, where as streams they come to a halt. Officially it is called "the psychic growing filth of the Dutch milieu." *"Psychic sewer"* of Europe is still only an underestimation for what is penetrating into schools, hospitals, churches and homes. Do you know that for instance the "Red book for pupils" has been written by teachers in Amsterdam of all places in the world? I shall not waste your time with more examples. The general idea why I mention this, is again the idea behind this book: *a people, like the Dutch, showing a strange resemblance with a tribe of Israel, Zebulun, when falling away from their Creator and from their true destiny, shown in the blessing, can turn such a blessing into a curse:*

Holland is nowadays flooded with rubbishy books in different "tongues" and here again we can point to some connections: it is becoming a filthy haven and refuge (reverse of Jacob) for suckers and milkers on psychic quicksand making big money, (reverse of Moses' sayings) grinning (instead of the beautiful word rejoicing!) when going out and calling the people towards Babel's tower, (instead of the Mountain Jerusalem) recruiting the younger generation by misusing their pen and the press, for a double-hearted insipid morality, which is the counterfeit of Zebulun's courageous men, who were "not of double heart."

As the counterpart of the extreme need for cleansing the polluted waters of Holland's haven, it is necessary to recruit forthwith a band of psychically cleansed Dutch Israelites, clean and clear of mind to excise the unclean spirits of Beelzebul from the House of Zebulun. You know who did it, the One who said: "I am the Light." Let in the inside of the houses and the souls of the people in Holland, the Light be lit again. Then they will be the first to set this example, as prophesied by Isaiah: *In the land of Zebulun light will spring up.*" (Matthew 4:16)

81

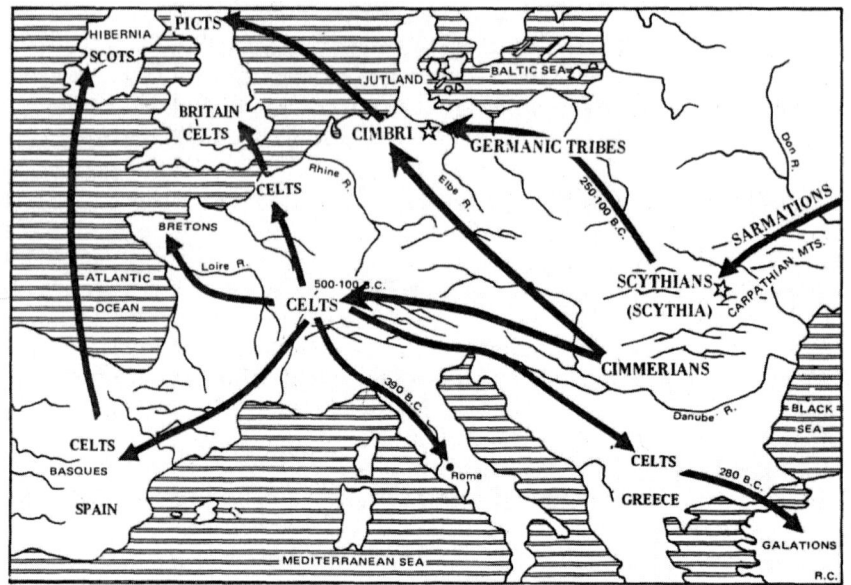

Cimmerians — Celtic tribes

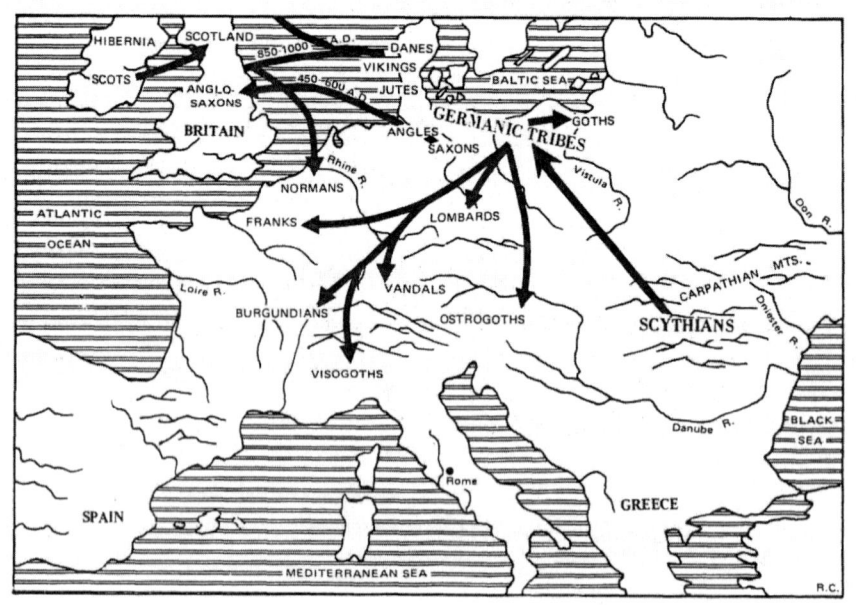

Scythians — Germanic tribes

# CHAPTER 12.

## ISAIAH'S PROPHECY FOR THE LAND OF ZEBULUN AND THE LIGHT IN THE NETHERLANDS.

"Nevertheless the dimness shall not be such as was in her vexation, when at first *he lightly afflicted the land of Zebulun...* and afterward did more grievously afflict her ( or *brought honor* ) *by way of the sea* (beyond Jordan in Galilee of the nations. *The people that walked in darkness have seen a great light.* They that dwell in the land of shadow and death, upon them has the light shined." (Isaiah 9 : 1) This reminds us of the fact that the land of Zebulun in latter days became part of Galilee.

This verse is always being cited at Christmas time, because it has foreseen the coming of the Messiah. Right, but have a closer look. Isaiah, Israel's greatest prophet and poet in the 8th century B.C. is speaking about the land of Zebulun and about its people. Where are they? As you know the Hebrew language had neither past nor future tense, it was always expressing itself in the present.

Isaiah has just witnessed the mass-deportation of the ten tribes of Israel, into Assyria. Among them is the tribe of Zebulun, never to return. They were not Jews, they were Israelites. Their tribe had grown to hundreds of thousands. Zebulun was afflicted and was thrown out of the Holy Land, wandering westward overland under other names such as the *Scyths, Sakka, Goths.* Historically nothing further is known about Zebulun's tribe. Undoubtedly however, skilled as they were at building ships and at seamanship they may have wandered westward mainly by way of the sea and by means of the old Mediterranean and Atlantic trade route; and by way of the great rivers of Europe to end up at the Rhine, Meuse and Scheldt-delta. Tracing Israel back to Western Europe has been done by others, but as far as to the Lowlands are concerned this study has still to be written. Suffice here to draw your attention to the possible historical backgrounds to our strange parallel between the deported and migrating Zebulunites and the early settlers in the Lowlands under names like *Kimren, Kelts,* and other pre-Roman peoples.

Is it so strange that the prophet is having two visions simultaneously? He sees the depopulated wasteland of Zebulun west of the river Jordan, where one day the Messiah will walk. He also sees the Zebulunites, afflicted by the sea in a land of dimness and darkness, seeing light.

## THE LOWLANDS AFFLICTED BY THE SEA

Is there any land in the western world that has had so many disastrous floods since times immemorial as the Netherlands? No regularly rising rivers here as in India, but sudden afflictions by a roaring and thundering sea attacking the land and its civilization. Legends tell us about dramatic disasters, one of them being called the *"Kimbrian flood"* of all names! More recently, in 1953 the land was afflicted more grievously. Was this applicable to Zebulun's land, which never bordered on the sea in Biblical times?* Orthodox Dutch fishermen and farmers at the latest disastrous breach of dykes cited this very verse of Isaiah when whole families in Zealand were drowned in the sea, fifteen hundred in one night, 1st of February, 1953. A people that fled in darkness on the top of their houses and saw the house-high waves running towards them. "In the land of shadow and death, upon them light has shined." To those among the Dutch who remember those days they themselves are the people of whom Isaiah spoke.

* It was promised to them, but they never inhabited the coastal region where Acco is now situated.

## TO BE HONORED AND GLORIFIED BY THE SEA

On another level, (both are right) there is the alternative translation which says that afterwards they were to be honored by the sea. Is there still an unfilled prophecy for the land of Zebulun? Some may regard the vast Netherlands' Delta works, which will eventually exclude the sea from the Delta, as a bearer of honors of the sea from all over the world to Dutch engineering skill.

How could the sea do honor and bring glory to a people that will hence forward be sitting in darkness? Thinking in terms of water, may the sea itself contain the elements for the purification of the water? What kind of food has the seawater in store for us? Are the Dutch heading for new inventions? The experiments made by the hydraulic laboratories at Delft in co-operation with Israeli engineers seem promising.

On yet another level of interpretation *the light of the Gospel* has been brought to these islands *by means of the sea* as early as A.D. 50 and again in the 5th and 6th centuries by Irish and English monks, long before Rome claims to have converted these barbarous and heathen "Germanic" tribes. This is a subject in itself. The *earliest missionaries to the Lowlands came in boats* and established centers along the coast of the Netherlands, "where the glory shone·" The abbey of Egmond (in Kennemerland, North Holland) and the Chronicle of Zealand by *Smallegange*, (A.D. 1696) whose historical views have been disputed, says that the Light shone here at the time of the apostles. Whether true or not it is a fact that recent archaeological findings concerning Nehalennia ( see page 61 ) confirm that a great international transit trade from the sea into the estuary of the Scheldt and Rhine in the Netherlands existed. Did the lost House of Israel see the light first in Zebulun, brought to them "by way of the sea?"

## LIGHT IN THE NETHERLANDS

Speaking about light in Zebulun, do you know that painters and photographers are always attracted by *the light in Holland*? Famous painters like Rembrandt, Vermeer, Pieter de Hoogh were reknowned for *painting of light*. Look at the pictures in the Rembrandt Bible.!

Why do they want to catch the ever changing light in Holland? Is there a symbol or a mystery behind the plain fact that the flat land with still standing waters, the white foam of the sea and the fair dunes function as a *mirror to reflect the light* of the ever changing sky? Incessantly clouds are forming over the Lowlands-delta, because the Netherlands form the bufferstate between the sea and the continent. The ever blowing wind in Holland plays a never ending game with these clouds causing an infinity of light and shadow-reflections on the reddish houses, the greenish land, the bluish waters, the yellowish sand dunes. The *silvery* interplay between water and sky in the Netherlands creates "it." It is this atmosphere which is called "typical Holland" for which artists and tourists still flock to this area, but... you don't go and see it from a touring car. Moreover the dirty ditches and filthy canals are rapidly ruining their fame of silvery shine nowadays.

Do you see how again a blessing and a curse intermingle? According to Isaiah, the blessing for Zebulun is, that the light will "spring up" there first. The blessing for the Netherlands with its

# V. HOOFTDEEL.

*Het Licht des Euangeliums is kort na d'Apostelen tyden in dese Landen opgegaen, en heeft daer ver...gens al heerlijk geschenen. Wat Willebrordus met de sijne, hier in g...a...n hebben?*

OM dat wy nu van de Tempelen en Afgoden des Heidendoms gesproken hebben, daer onse Vooroude-ren door hare blindheit in saten, soo dunkt het ons niet ongeraden hiert'onderfoekken wanneer de Christelijke Religie in dese Landen bekent is geworden. Aengaende de gene die aldereerst het Christelijk Geloof in onse Landen gebragt hebben, lefen wy in den tweeden *Sendbrief Pauls tot Timotheum*, het 4. cap. het 10. vers: *Crefcens na Galauen.* *Eufebius* noemt het Gallien; waer van wy voor een gedeelte zijn erkent. *Nicephorus* feit; *Dat Symon Zelotes in vele Landen ge-predikt hebbende, ten laesten de leere des Euan-geliums heeft overgedragen tot den westelijken* Oceaan, en de Brittannische Eylanden. *Joseph* van *Arimathea* was door *Philippus* uit Gallien na Brittannien over-gesonden; gelijk *Polidorus Virgilius*, *Hosius*, en andere getuigen.

*Joseph lib. 2. cap. 40.*
*Hof.Cem. I. lib. 2. cap. 10.*

Wy vinden in de levens der Biffchoppen van Tongeren, welker Stoel naderhand binnen Luyck is overgebragt, dat ontrent het jaer 50. na de geboorte onfes Saligmakers, drie Apoftelijke Mannen, *Eucharius*, *Vale-rius*, en *Maternus*, door den heiligen Apoftel *Petrus*, naer het Belgijs-Gaulen gefon-den zijn, die tot Trier, Tungren, Luyck, en Keulen, de gronden der Christelijke Religie gelegt, en het vruchtbaer zaed des Goddelijken woords rijkkelijk zaejende, vele

*Harige-rus, Abb Lob. du gestis Tungr, & Leod.cap 5, 7.&c*

clean havens and natural waters has always been that it was a country of light. This involves the parallel curse that Holland is rapidly cursing itself as a light, enlightened country by polluting its water, its air, its people, so that the people will live in darkness and in a never changing sort of thick dimness of the sky. The smooth mirror of Holland is becoming dingy and almost everywhere the dim polluted atmosphere does no longer show silvery light.

Do reflect on this blessing and curse and all its possible consequences. The Dutch as a people of Israel have the free will to turn the day and the land may still become an example. If we draw the parallel to the end, then *the Netherlands will see the light first.*

## THE LIGHT TO COME WITHIN THE HOMES.

A young man, six feet (almost two meters) tall, with hazel brown hair over his shoulders, and irresistable steel-blue eyes (see letter Publius Lentulus) suddenly appeared and "sprang up" in Galilee, being the land of Zebulun, saying "I am the Light." He came straight to the land of Zebulun after he had been tempted in the desert to bow for Beelzebul and his friends. What does John say? "Turn back, for the Kingdom is at hand." (Matthew 3:2). What does he do? In the land of Zebulun he begins by healing the possessed. He casts the friends of Beelzebul out into swines which kill themselves. I am not trying to preach. These are hard actual facts. He is the Way and the Light. There is no other one to be followed.

CHRIST IN GALILEE (ZEBULUN)

## THE STRANGE PARALLEL BECOMES A TRUE PARALLEL.

Holland, country of light, has to be cleansed first from its sickness, in order to become Zebulun, the dwelling of the elevated. If it is true the destruction will come by fire to many parts of the earth, the atmosphere will be so dim and dark that the sun will be blackened. When this will come, says the Bible "go into your dwellings and wait." There will be light inside. There will be light in each inner home that has been cleansed. As it was in Moses' time when Egypt sat in darkness, while the Israelites were surrounded by the Shekinah-light, so it will be in times to come — Zebulun will see the light first. Those in the Netherlands, who are aware that this strange parallel is a true one, will behave as children of Zebulun. Being cleansed, they will dwell safely, and they will receive the grace of seeing the return of the Light.

## A RISEN LOWLAND, AN ELEVATED ZEBULUN,

## ONE DELIGHTFUL PEOPLE, INDWELLED BY HIS LIGHT.

"What then of these people, these north-western Europeans living in the flat lands of Holland? Are they descended through the ages from the People of Zebulun? If they be of Zebulun, then they are of Israel. Down the long corridors of time, past the 20th century, the prophets foresaw a wondrous future, for Zebulun, as Isaiah foretold, would see the LIGHT FIRST."

# „ZEBULON"-HYMNE

### Lofzang aan de God van Israël

Tekst en Muziek
NIEK SCHEPS

1. Het gro - te Licht dat 't eerst van al in Ze - bu - lon ver - schij - nen zal, komt
hen die in het duis - ter staan, ver - los sen uit hun dood en waan. Ze - bu - lon, Ze - bu - lon zal
wo - nen in het Licht. ___ Ze - bu - lon, Ze - bu - lon zal wo - nen in het Licht.

† met het heilige vuur der bezieling.

This Zebulun Hymn is now available as a 10 min. colour film (8 mm and 16 mm), illustrating the text and sung by Dutch choirs (with English subtitles) Real Israel Press – 55 Hill Head, Glastonbury, Somerset, Great Britain.

# ZEBULON HYMN

## Song of Praise to the God of Israel

### Words and music by Nicholas Scheps ©

1. To Zebulon enwrapped in night
Shall first return His wondrous Light,
Our deathdark thoughts He casts away
That we may live in light each day.
Zebulon, Zebulon shall dwell within His Light.

2. In Galilee in Zebulon
The Lord His Ministry began,
The water changed to wedding wine,
My Father's Kingdom shall be thine'.
Zebulon, Zebulon shall dwell within His Light.

   In Galilea – Zebulon
   ontspringt het Licht als Levensbron,
   het water wordt tot bruiloftswijn:
   ,,Gods Koninkrijk zal bij U zijn!''
   Zebulon, Zebulon zal wonen in het Licht. (2x)

3. And Moses blesses Zebulon :
'Suck thou th'abundance of the seas
And treasures hidden in the sand,
Abundance both of sea and land'.
Zebulon, Zebulon shall dwell within His Light.

   En Mozes ziet dat Zebulon
   zich voeat met wat de zee hem biedt
   en schatten opzuigt uit het zand:
   een overvloed uit zee en land.
   Zebulon, Zebulon zal wonen in het Licht (2x)

4. 'Rejoice then in thy going out,
Call all men to the Holy Mount,
Proclaim His message far and wide,
Set thou thy gifts upon His side .
Zebulon, Zebulon shall dwell within His Light.

   Verheug U in Uw zendingswerk,
   de volken roepend tot de berg,
   gij schrijft Gods boodschap wereldwijd,
   brengt offers in rechtvaardigheid,
   Zebulon, Zebulon zal wonen in het Licht (2x)

5. From storms a haven to maintain,
The open sea thy ship's domain,
Thy staunch sons braving wind and tide,
Their nets thrown out on either side.
Zebulon, Zebulon shall dwell within His Light

   Zijn land zal tot een haven zijn,
   de wijde zee zijn visdomein,
   zijn zonen vissen frank en vrij
   hun netten vol aan beide zij.
   Zebulon, Zebulon zal wonen in het Licht (2x)

6. Thus blesses Jacob Zebulon,
Long ere the Great Exile began.
This blessing gave to Zebulon,
These sea-washed coasts to dwell upon.
Zebulon, Zebulon shall dwell within His Light.

   Zó zegent Jacob Zebulon
   lang vóór de ballingschap begon,
   zijn zegen bracht hij met zich mee
   toen hij ging wonen langs de zee.
   Zebulon, Zebulon zal wonen in het Licht (2x)

7. The Holy Spirit led us here
With open hearts all Thine we are,
Our prayer to Thee, Emmanuel,
'Bring Light t'all tribes of Israel !'
Zebulon, Zebulon shall dwell within His Light.

   Hier staan wij, door Uw geest geleid,
   met open hart U toegewijd,
   wij bidden U, Immanuël:
   verlicht Uw donker Israël!
   Zebulon, Zebulon zal wonen in het Licht. (2x)

8. If we our ancestry will hail.
Turn back to God as Israel,
Then Zebulon the first shall see
His radiant Light to set them free.
Zebulon, Zebulon shall dwell within His Light.

   Wanneer dit volk zichzelf herkent,
   als Israël tot God zich wendt,
   mag Zebulon het eerst van al
   de Heer zien Die dán komen zal.
   Zebulon, Zebulon zal wonen in het Licht (2x)

9. Twelve thousand out of Zebulon
Arise before His Lightning Throne,
Extol the Lamb and praise His Name.
All Israel a golden flame.
Israel, Israel shall dwell within His Light.

   Dán zal ook Zebulon eens gaan
   met twaalf maal duizend juichend staan,
   Héél Israël zal door het Lam
   gaan lichten als een gouden vlam.
   Israël, Israël zal wonen in het Licht (2x)

7. Nu staan wij, Heer, dicht bij Uw zee*)
en vieren Uw geboorte mee.*)

## HELENE W. KOPPEJAN
*( Helene W. van Woelderen )*

Helene was born August 20, 1927 by the river Scheldt on the 'boulevard' of Flushing, Zealand. She was the burgomaster's daughter and descended on her mother's side from French Huguenots, who fled to Middelburg in the 16th century, where they made their fortunes in the wool trade; as partners in the Dutch East India Company, and, (oh brother) by selling slaves, which did not seem to clash with their Calvinistic principles of freedom.

On her father's side there were some generations of Dutch Reformed clergymen, who introduced "Israel Daniel" as a family name. None of her forebears however gave the slightest hint of having known of Holland being literally Israel. Helene had to find this out entirely on her own, though her father, when alive was a scholar of Dutch history and a writer about genealogy and heraldry.

She went to the "Latin School" (where she had to learn six languages) in Middelburg during the second World War on the island of Walcheren on the Scheldt estuary, this being the most attacked spot of Holland during World War II ranging from the burning of Middelburg by the Germans, bombing by the Allied, to being entirely flooded as part of the war-strategy of the battle of the Scheldt in 1944. The island of Walcheren was the first Dutch territory to be liberated by the Scottish Lowlanders (52nd Division) and the British 4th Commandos. The device of Zealand is a lion emerging from the water with the words "luctor et emergo," I struggle and emerge. It is small wonder that Helene chose the start of Strange Parallel on the island of Walcheren.

93

Helene studied sociology and psychology during seven years at the University of Amsterdam and graduated in what is now called "andragogie," meaning behaviour of man; a study which means nothing when forgetting that man is not guiding and going himself but with the Holy Spirit and the Will of the God of Israel. That she had to learn for herself sometimes the hard way.

1957-'58 she went to the United States for a scholarship being promised to her, which never turned up. Returning home, she established a free-lance practice in the field of vocational guidance, mainly in the Hague. With her late husband, Willem A. Koppejan she wrote a book; J.B. Nicklin, "A Life with God and the Pyramid," which they published as Trustees of the Real Israel Press Charity Foundation. This they initiated in order to give further publicity to their joined conviction that their future years would be devoted to putting into print any idea which is furthering the identification of Real (in the sense of true) Israel.

They named their second home in Glastonbury: Zebulun Hove. Helene's articles about subjects related to the present book were published in Identity (Vancouver, Canada), The National Message, (London) Nieuw Geluid (Mijdrecht, Netherlands), and many other publications.

Address:

Zebulun-Hove,
55 Hill Head,
Glastonbury.
Somerset (BA6 8AW) Great Britain

# Bibical texts in which Zebulun is mentioned

| Genesis | 30 : 20 | birth and namegiving |
|---|---|---|
| | 35 : 23 | brothers of Zebulun (sons of Leah) |
| | 46 : 14 | sons of Zebulun |
| | 49 : 13 | blessing of Jacob to his son Zebulun |
| Exodus | 1 : 3 | Zebulun in Egypt |
| Numeri | 1 : 9 | Names of officers in Zebulun |
| | 1 : 31, 2 : 7-8 | Numbering the soldiers of Zebulun |
| | 1 : 26-30 | Zebulun between Judah and Issaschar in the armies of Israel |
| | 7 : 24-29 | offerings by the princes of Zebulun |
| | 10 : 16 | tribe of Zebulun under the standard of Judah |
| | 13 : 10 | a spy for Canaan of the tribe of Zebulun |
| | 26 : 26-27 | Sons of Zebulun |
| | 34 : 25 | the prince of Zebulun who will divide the land |
| Deuter-onomy | 27 : 13 | Zebulun will curse on Mount Ebal |
| | 33 : 18-19 | blessing of Moses to the tribe of Zebulun |
| Joshua | 19: 10, 16, 27, 34 | partition of the land for the children of Zebulun according to lot |
| | 21 : 7, 34-35 | twelve cities of Zebulun, their names, |
| | 21 : 35 | Nahalal |
| Judges | 1 : 30 | Zebulun does not drive out the Canaanites |
| | 4 : 6, 10 | Deborah gathers Zebulun to fight against Sisera |
| | 5 : 14, 18 | blessing of Deborah to the children of Zebulun |
| | 6 : 35 | Gideon sends messengers unto Zebulun |
| | 12 : 12 | the judge Elon, the Zebulunite dies and is buried in the country of Zebulun |
| 1 Chronicles | 2 : 1 | Zebulun among the sons of Israel |
| | 6 : 63, 77 | twelve cities of Zebulun |
| | 12 : 33 | Zebulunites who were not of double heart |
| | 12 : 40 | eating and drinking with David for three days |
| | 27 : 19 | name of captain over Zebulun |
| 2 Chronicles | 30 : 10, 11 | divers of Zebulun humbled themselves |
| | 20 : 18 | Zebulun had not cleansed themselves |
| Psalm | 68 : 27 | Princes of Zebulun |
| Isaiah | 9 : 1 | prophecy of Isaiah for the land of Zebulun, the light |
| Ezekiel | 48 : 26, 27, 33 | new division of the land |
| Matthew | 4 : 13, 15 | fulfillment of Isaiah's prophecy for the land of Zebulun |
| | 10 : 25 | Beelzebul 1) |
| Revelation | 7 : 8 | 12,000 of the tribe of Zebulun sealed |

1

Beelzebul is Aramaic. Beelzebub (as it is often spelt) means: *the Lord of the flies* (2 Kings 1, 2), and was the god of the Ekronites. This name was changed by the Israelites as a " symbolic pun " to Baalzebul - *Lord of the dungeon or household*, hence used as prince of the demons.

# BIBLIOGRAPHY and Suggestions for further reading

I have abstained from giving the main bulk of Dutch references which are inaccessible to English readers. There is a vast literature about the Netherlands, which is available in any library.
A few related books in English mentioned in the text are:

**Green, Lawrence:**
Almost forgotten, never told, 1965, Howard Timmins, Capetown, South Africa. With a chapter on the Flying Dutchman, ghostship of the Cape.

**Hondius-Crone, A.:**
The Temple of Nehalennia at Domburg, Meulenhoff, Amsterdam, 1955. An archeological study dating from before the recent findings, best study on the subject in English.

**Jenkins. F.:**
Nameless or Nehalennia, Archaeologia Cantiana 70, 1957, pgs. 192-200, attempting to identify discoveries at Canterbury with Nehalennia.

**Milner, W. M. H.:**
The Royal House of Britain, an enduring Dynasty, 1964 ed. at Covenant Books, 6 Buckingham Gate, London S.W.1, with a genealogy including Ratherius of Rotterdam.

**Wilson, John:**
Lectures on our Israelitish Origin, 1876 ed. (fifth) at James Nisbet, London, 442 pg. (antiquarian).

**Wilson, Charles:**
The Dutch Republic, 1968, World University Library, Weidenfeld and Nicholson, London, 255 pages. Description of Holland in the 17th century, the growth of its unique economy, its influence on European ideas of trade, art, science, literature and philosophy. Recommended.

**The Companion Bible:**
1964 edition, Samuel Bagster & Sons, London, being the authorised version of the Bible in 1611.

**James Strong:**
Exhaustive Concordance of the Bible, 27th edition 1967, Hodder & Stoughton Ltd., London.

**Testament of the twelve Patriarchs:**
Edited by R. H. Charles, Society of Promoting Christian Knowledge, London. 1st edition 1917, 2nd edition 1925. A translation of an apocryphal book with the full text of the words spoken by the Sons of Jacob on their successive deathbed.